MAIDEN, MOTHER, CRONE

VOICES OF THE GODDESS

CLAIRE HAMILTON

Copyright © 2005 O Books
O Books is an imprint of John Hunt Publishing Ltd., The Bothy,
Deershot Lodge, Park Lane, Ropley, Hants, SO24 0BE, UK
office@johnhunt-publishing.com
www.O-books.net

Distribution in:
UK
Orca Book Services
orders@orcabookservices.co.uk
Tel: 01202 665432 Fax: 01202 666219 Int. code (44)

USA and Canada
NBN
custserv@nbnbooks.com
Tel: 1 800 462 6420 Fax: 1 800 338 4550

Australia
Brumby Books
sales@brumbybooks.com
Tel: 61 3 9761 5535 Fax: 61 3 9761 7095

New Zealand
Peaceful Living
books@peaceful-living.co.nz
Tel: 64 7 57 18105 Fax: 64 7 57 18513

Singapore
STP
davidbuckland@tlp.com.sg
Tel: 65 6276 Fax: 65 6276 7119

South Africa
Alternative Books
altbook@global.co.za
Tel: 27 011 792 7730 Fax: 27 011 972 7787

Text: © Claire Hamilton 2005

Design of text and cover: BookDesign™, London
Cover painting: "Metamorphosis" by Terri Windling,
www.endicott-studio.com

ISBN 1 905047 39 8

A CIP catalogue record for this book is available from the
British Library.

Printed in the USA by Maple-Vail Manufacturing Group

MAIDEN, MOTHER, CRONE

VOICES OF THE GODDESS

CLAIRE HAMILTON

BOOKS

WINCHESTER UK
NEW YORK USA

To Steve, my Manawydan.
Also to Rosa, the babe in the cauldron.

ACKNOWLEDGEMENTS

Many have lent their energies to this book, in particular, my support group: Lyndsay, Desdemona, and my sister Rosie. Also Debbie Johnson, my mentor and one-time tutor. Besides these close women friends there are many others whose energies have crept into the book, and to whom I am very grateful. I was very privileged in being commissioned to write this book for, throughout its writing, I worked with each goddess personally and was challenged, empowered and blessed by each in turn. It has been an amazing journey for me, and one that I would like others to share. It is therefore my passionate hope that all who read the tales of these extraordinary goddesses will be as touched, empowered and blessed as I have been in the writing of it.

VOICES OF THE GODDESS
CD

Claire Hamilton has set the poems and
meditations in this book to music and
recorded an album of pieces that reflect the
gifts and characteristics of each of the
goddesses. The album is a wonderful
accompaniment to the book, using the
power of music, word and Celtic harp as a
powerful aide in invoking and meditating
on the gifts of each goddess. For details
please visit Claire's website:
www.livingmyths.com

CONTENTS

INTRODUCTION

THE GODDESS is coming back! She is returning in myriad ways, some subtle, others less so. More obviously she is returning in the rising power of women in the workplace, politics and the Church. Subtly she is returning through myth, magic and intuition. But who is she and where does she come from? Is she a deity, a historical ruler, an idea, a principle or an archetype?

Perhaps the first place to look for the goddess is back in time. Our culture has long been acquainted with the Greek goddesses and we are now becoming more aware of Middle Eastern and even Hindu ones. All these goddesses are powerful and commanding and many people are revisiting their stories. Yet what about our own heritage? What has happened to the Celtic goddesses that once walked our own land? These goddesses had the closest involvement with the people of Great Britain and much of Europe. It was once believed they brought us help, guidance, strength, wisdom and understanding. But then they suddenly disappeared. They were overturned, pushed underground, buried and forgotten. Yet now they are returning. Brighid, Deirdre, Branwen, Rhiannon, Arianrhod … their names are becoming familiar again.

But their stories are not so familiar. This is because, after they were recorded by monks in the Middle Ages, they remained untranslated until the 19th century, and since then have mostly been confined to awkward and dry versions. They therefore lack the refinement of the Greek myths, which were rewritten by Homer. But they deserve to be better known, for they are extraordinary tales – provocative and surprising, as are the goddesses themselves.

The Celtic goddesses offer a fascinating and unique expression of the Great Goddess as ancient deity. Although they share many of the attributes of the goddesses from other cultures – for example, in being linked to the fertility of the earth, there are some important and valuable differences, especially when they are compared to the Greek deities. For, unlike the Greek goddesses, who were usually defined by role, the Celtic goddesses were multi-functional. Thus The Morrigan was the goddess of sex as well as of war and death, and Brighid represented fertility as well as healing, poetry and smithcraft. Yet, although their roles often overlapped, these goddesses were powerful figures in their own right. Not only that, they were multi-faceted, being able to encompass both the dark and light sides of life, and to preside simultaneously over death and life, war and peace, love and loss. In other words, they were able to turn with the seasons and reflect the different faces of nature.

Their link with the seasons was very important. For, to the Celts, as with many other cultures, the Goddess was the embodiment of nature, the eternal force that held everything in balance. It was she who held in her hands the key to the mysteries of life and death, she who carried the knowledge of the unknown. And it was she who was able to go down into the darkness of winter and rise again with the spring.

It was because of this that Robert Graves in 'The White Goddess' put forward the idea of her having three distinct faces: Mother, Bride and Layer-out. These, he felt, corresponded to the seasons of spring, summer and winter. Grave's idea has since been embraced and the three phases re-named Maiden, Mother and Crone. Besides representing the seasons they are also linked to the three phases of the moon – waxing, full and waning, and to the three key stages in a woman's life – youth, motherhood and old age. Whether this concept is of ancient origin or not, it provides an excellent framework for the role of the goddess as perceived in the Celtic myths.

As to whether the goddess is a historical figure, many believe that among most ancient civilizations there was once a golden age of

Matriarchal rule. This belief is supported by archaeological finds of thousands of early female fertility figurines, and very few male ones. The theory is that early societies worshipped a Mother Goddess – perhaps linked with her dying and rising son, and that such civilizations were agriculturally based, peaceful and democratic. Evidence from the myths also supports this, since many of them depict conflict between Matriarchal and Patriarchal ideologies. They also chart a growing disrespect and disregard for female power.

But whether such a society existed historically or not, the idea or concept of the divine feminine is certainly of ancient origin. In Greek philosophy she was known as Sophia, the spirit of wisdom. She also appears in the Old Testament. 'She is more precious than jewels, and nothing you desire can compare with her,' says the Book of Proverbs.

In early Christian times the Gnostics regarded her as the mystical aspect of the godhead, the original female principle or 'the great invisible virgin spirit'. They also considered the Holy Spirit to be female and connected her to the idea of the 'Word' in St John's Gospel. Similar views are also found in Eastern mystery religions. In Sufism, for example, she is referred to as the Divine Mystery, or 'Veiled Idea'.

But, in the west, after the beliefs of the Gnostics were pronounced heretical and outlawed by the Roman Church, the idea of the Divine Feminine was forced underground. Instead of being acknowledged openly she was carried in the powerful symbolism of the Holy Grail of the Arthurian legends and worshipped in secret sects such as those of the Knight's Templar. In terms of organized religion, the only figure that remained to represent her was that of the Virgin Mary. Yet, although the deified figure of the Virgin Mary carried the Maiden and Mother aspects of the original Goddess, that of the Crone was distinctly lacking.

It was not until the advent of psychology in the twentieth century that the hidden idea of the goddess was openly revisited. Carl Jung, who was a pioneer in this field, posited the idea of the 'collective unconscious', a universal pool of symbolic material lying behind and beyond the individual unconscious. His studies revealed an imbalance in the psyche of modern man – which prompted an examination of the feminine principle. Broadly speaking, Jung divided the psyche into two parts, consciousness or *logos*, which he considered 'masculine' and the unconscious, or *mythos*, which he considered 'feminine'. Jung believed that the principle of the Eternal Feminine was buried in the collective unconscious. He called it an archetype, an innate force whose function was to organize the individual unconscious and to bring about balance within the psyche.

But to Jung the concepts of masculine and feminine were not gender-specific. They could equally be defined as left-brain and right-brain thinking. To him, therefore, the return of the goddess denoted the return of the feminine principle in a world that had become too much concerned with rational thinking.

But Jung was not the only one who perceived this imbalance. Graves also called for the return of the feminine approach to life. He defined the opposing principles in these terms: 'There are two distinct and complementary languages; the ancient, intuitive language of poetry …. and the more modern, rational language or prose, universally current.' Like Jung, Graves also believed that the feminine principle could not be accessed by reason or logic but only through dream and symbol.

Both men also believed that the archetypes were expressed in myths and that therefore myths could be used to access them. Jung, in particular, saw myths as representing the individual's journey towards psychic wholeness.

Since Jung, many other great thinkers have followed this path. The work of men such as James Hillman and Joseph Campbell has helped to open up the riches of the unconscious even further. Both men continued Jung's idea of working with myths on a personal level to facilitate individual development. In fact the claims Joseph Campbell made for the importance of myth could hardly be higher: 'Myth,' he said, 'touches what is ultimate in man and in his life, expresses it symbolically, and provides an inner perspective by which the mysteries of human existence are felt and entered into.'

Such claims are hardly too high. For mythology is a powerful and magical tool, one that has withstood the test of time, that speaks of unfathomable wisdom, that can help to usher in the feminine principle and provide a gateway to the soul. For, at the heart of the mystery of human existence lies the unknown, the numinous, the inexpressible. It is the figure of the eternal Goddess, standing quietly at the threshold, and holding in her hand the fruits and riches of the inner life.

Claire Hamilton

PROLOGUE

The voice of the Goddess spoke the first word. But it was not a word. It was an impulse, a thought, a quickening.

For the voice of the Goddess is subtle. It speaks in image, metaphor, poem, symbol. It can be heard on the wind, felt in the touch of grass, tasted in a squeeze of fruit, or smelled like a waft of fragrance shaken from a bush.

She is difficult to hear for her voice is elusive. It will not speak in straight lines. It shuns logic and defies reason.

Yet it spins and sings within each woman and man – a still small voice, a shiver of intuition, a whispered wisdom.

These tales of the Celtic Goddess are told in her own voice. She reveals her wisdom and expresses her truths through metaphor, myth, poetry, image and symbol. She shares her strengths, her hopes, her loves, her pain, her trials, her burdens and her sorrows. She reveals her dark powers as well as her bright ones. Sometimes she speaks as the Maiden, sometimes as the Mother and sometimes as the Crone. In this she follows both her own fate and the turning of the year. For she embodies the land.

In her Maiden aspect she represents springtime. This is when she emerges from the dark of winter and arrives to wake the earth. Her role is to renew the fertility of the land, tease out its shoots, raise its buds and its vegetation, inspire its crops and fruitfulness.

In her Mother aspect she represents summer and autumn. This is the time when she bears her child. Her role is to nurture growth, to encourage the fruition of the land and the harvesting of crops.

In her Crone aspect she represents winter. This is the barren time when she withdraws from the earth and goes into the darkness, the time when she tastes death and learns its wisdom.

Then the wheel turns and next spring she returns, young, fresh, beautiful, renewed...

MAIDEN
GODDESSES

MAIDEN

IN HER Maiden aspect the Goddess is young, pliant, sure of herself. In these tales we see the Maiden archetype defining herself within the conditions of society, especially its masculine values. So, instead of meek, biddable virgin figures, we find powerful young women challenging their limitations. They obey their inner natures rather than bowing to authority. Through their defiance and refusal to conform, these Maiden goddesses can release valuable blessings on the earth. Also, through their strength of will and self-belief they become symbols of hope.

The voice of the Maiden is in the stir of the shoot,
the unfolding of petal and leaf,
the greening of bough and branch.

It is the voice of one who dreams the land,
who pulses with the earth
whose veins flow with the sap of life.

The voice of one who flames
with the fires of life,
who matches her steps to the ritual dance,
and treads the eternal round.

BRIGHID THE MAIDEN

I, BRIGHID, am older than time itself and young as the earliest day of spring. I am *breo-saigit*, the shining one, a fiery arrow. My hair blazes from my head. My robes are white as the sudden snowdrops that spring up wherever I put my feet. I am a goddess of fire. I hang my cloak to dry upon the shafts of the sun. I inspire the smith, forging his magic weapons in the burning flames. I inspire the poets, forging their words within the fires of creation. I inspire the physician in the subtle arts of healing. I am a threefold goddess.

The powers of fire and water are in my hands. I stand at the place where three streams meet. I come, pale out of the new sky, tender as the newborn lambs, my breasts milk-white. I come at Imbolc and wake the sleeping earth. I breathe life into the cave-black mouth of winter.

My hair is like the sun's bright strands. I walk the cold earth and bless the warm hearth's glow.

> *Hail reign a fair maid with gold upon your toe,*
> *Open up the West Gate and let the Old Year go.*

In the quiet, hidden place the still well waits for me. I blow softly on its shining waters.

> *Hail reign a fair maid with gold upon your chin,*
> *Open up the East Gate and let the New Year in.*

I wear a crown of candles, their flames spiralling into the darkness.

I am a queen of making.

> *Levideu sing Levideu the water and the wine,*
> *The seven bright gold wires and the candles that do shine.*

For I am the white maid of the early spring – the goddess of hope and promise, treading the fields when the lambs struggle in the frozen dawn. I am also the yielding flow, the sweet warm ewes' milk that sustains and comforts them.

Spring Maiden, Virgin Goddess am I, giving my name to brides in their milky, snowdrop gowns.

But I am also Mother and Wise-woman, protector and counsellor, bestowing on the earth bright blessings from the dawning sun.

Brighid of the mantles,
Brighid of the peat-heap
Brighid of the twining hair
Brighid of the augury.
Brighid of the white feet,
Brighid of calmness,
Brighid of the white palms,
Brighid of the kine.

Brighid, my comrade-woman
Brighid, my maker of song,
Brighid, my helping-woman
My choicest of women, my guide.

BLODEUWEDD

FROM THE dreamtime I was called. Summoned by the wands of Math and Gwydion. At first their call was faint, so faint. A sigh in my ivy hair, a leaf-shift. Who was it called me from my slumber? My fingers were delved deep into the earth, snake-wriggling below the trunks of trees. My hair a flung green web, draping the fallen branches. It was hard to raise myself, hard to answer my summoning.

But the call grew stronger. The sweet magic of it danced like birdsong on my limbs and, all at once, I knew it was the call of man.

I tried to resist. But the man's strong spell was on me, pulling up my roots, plucking at my hair, raising me from the time of sleep and dreaming. And so, summoned by scented oak smoke, crush of meadowsweet and broom, I came.

The two men had prepared a body for me. All I had to do was step inside. Soft-spreading leaves, fine-branched twigs and downy petals whirled into harmony as I entered. Breath of breeze was waiting, glaze of dew, flame-flick of power to shake me into being.

As I spiralled into life I saw the two magicians looking at me. The young one's blue eyes compelled me. I saw a light in them, the light of craft. I felt the ecstasy shoot through him, the ecstasy of raising me to life – or so he thought. But the older mage had a different power. His hands moved with authority, his wand work was deft, accomplished. It was their twin magic that had sealed my fate.

I stretched my arms and felt the cracking of the twigs. Leaf-dust shimmered from me as I moved my lithe body. My hair fell free when I shook it. A sound came from my mouth, a trickling laugh like sprinkled water. I took a step and faltered. My feet were not yet strong, the power had not yet settled in me. As I stumbled, Gwydion, the young one, reached out his arm and caught me. He held me to his heart, but carefully for he feared to crush me. The beat of his heart was loud. It thudded through my new-made form, awaking my strength. All the while, Math, the old one, regarded me from afar, his hands stroking his beard, up and down, up and down, his grey eyes large with wonder.

As soon as I was strong enough, I was taken to Lleu Llaw Gyffes, my future husband. He stared at me in awe. To him I was a crafted creature, beautifully finished. I smiled prettily and tossed my hair, which made him entranced. King of the sun was he, lord of the shining spear. I could have married worse.

The wedding was a glittering affair. Lleu, they said, was radiant with love. I was honoured for my perfect features, my untouched beauty. During the feast Gwydion turned to Math and said cunningly:

'It is not easy for a man without land to support himself.'

Math considered this. Then he raised his goblet and eyed Gwydion over the rim.

'Very well,' he said at last, 'I will bestow on him the best province he could possibly have!'

'Which one is that?'

'Ardudwy,' Math answered.

Gwydion sat back in his chair, content.

So, after the wedding feast, we departed for Ardudwy. Lleu set up court in a castle in the hills. He ruled the land from there and our people were content.

But I was not.

At first I did not know what troubled me. Our life was orderly, everything paced according to the hour. Lleu was fair-minded and punctilious. He was kind to me, affectionate, but his touch was light. All was brightness with him. As the new sun stretched its arms across the sky, Lleu stretched himself and rose from our bed before the day grew warm.

I remember the day he planned to visit Math I was particularly restless. It was spring. The shoots were breaking through the earth, tendrils of new and fragile blossoms were unfolding. I felt a stirring deep within my veins. I turned about the court. A deep magic was taking hold. If Lleu noticed, he said nothing. I wanted him to stay with me. But his heart was set upon the journey.

After he'd gone, my restlessness grew stronger. Again and again I sighed and turned about the court. Then I went outside and walked about on the ramparts of the castle. I looked out over the forest. I could feel the flap of bird, the scuffling of mole and badger. I could sense the wild creatures edging towards each other, driven by the relentless ritual, preparing to create their young.

As I looked out, I heard the blare of a horn and saw a commotion in the forest. Then, suddenly, a stag burst through the branches fleeing for its life, but tiring and stumbling, no longer neat-footed. And then the hunter came in sight. How fast he was! How lissome, leaping between the trees!

I followed the stag and the man with fascinated eyes until they were swallowed by the forest. Then I sent a servant to enquire after the hunter.

After a while the man returned, breathless.

'Well, what is his name?' I asked.

'Gronwy the Staunch, Lord of Penllyn,' he replied.

I went indoors after that. But my restlessness only grew more intense. I paced the chambers of the court until evening. Then, just before the hour of feasting, I went out on the parapet again. As I gazed at the dusk-draped woodland, I saw a lone figure coming towards the castle gate.

'It would be rank discourtesy to let this great lord pass our gate at such an hour and not offer him hospitality,' I said to my servants.

'It would indeed,' they replied.

So I ordered them to invite him in.

II

I WENT down to the gate myself to greet the hunter. His clothes were gashed from the chase, earth was on his hands and streaks of blood on his clothes from flailing the stagskin. He looked at me through a web of wet hair.

'May the gods reward you, Lady, for your welcome,' he said.

I ordered the servants to take him to a guest chamber where he bathed and was given a change of clothes.

When he came in to dine, I noticed he was wearing Lleu's tunic. It sat well on him. His black hair was unruly, stray locks were still hanging over his face, but his skin shone and his eyes were intense behind the hair.

I was held all evening by the power of his gaze. Throughout our meal he treated me as if I were the first shoot of the spring, the first female he had seen in all his life. He ate with relish, tearing the fowl with his teeth, and the wildness in him caught at my heart and called to the essence of me. We laughed together. Our hands skimmed against each other. We drank carelessly, meeting one another's eyes over the flashing goblets. We drank in gladness and celebration, our minds, our souls, our bodies helplessly inflamed.

That night he lay with me. I had known no other man but Lleu, and Lleu had no other choice but me. But this man was my choice and I was his. This wild man, flushed with drink, running his huntsman's hands across my white flesh, this man who drank and swore and took no heed of the hour, whose laughter filled the chamber and whose eyes spiralled into darkness. This unfathomable man speared me with his passion, and we trembled together in the force of our love.

Next morning, Gronwy gathered up his hunting gear and prepared to leave. I flew to him and stretched my arms around him. I tipped back my head and felt the sweetness of his mouth on the white skin of my neck.

'By all the gods,' I said, 'I will not let you leave me tonight.'

'Then I will not go,' he said.

That night we declared our love. We were caught in a whorl of passion. Never had I felt such vibrancy, it seemed as if the entire thrust of spring was humming in my body. There was no beginning or ending between us, nor did we wish for any.

'I cannot let you go,' I said.

'Nor I you,' he replied.

My eyes were luminous with unspilled tears.

'But how can we stay together?'

When I said these words Gronwy turned away. His eyes blackened as he stared out at the forest.

'There is only one way,' he said quietly.

A rush of hope stabbed through me. I raised myself on my elbow and bent over him.

'What is that?'

He looked up at me. His eyes were dull.

'We shall have to discover how he can be killed.'

In the silence that fell between us we were both thinking the same thing - there was a spell that encircled Lleu and could guard his life forever. We would have to discover what it was, and break it.

As if he could read my thoughts Gronwy said: 'You will have to find it out. You can do it under pretence of anxiety.'

I said nothing, but I felt afraid.

Next morning, I again begged him to stay. But we both knew it was risky, for he would be in danger if Lleu returned.

'I will let you leave tomorrow,' I said.

The next day I helped him gather up his hunting gear. We clung together in a last embrace. Then I let him go.

That night Lleu returned. He seemed pleased to see me and we spent the next day together, singing and carousing. He told me of his visit to Math and his time at the court. But I looked at him, the man I had been created to love, and felt no passion for him.

That night when we went to bed I was silent. When Lleu spoke to me I did not answer.

'Are you all right?' he asked. 'Has anything happened?'

I turned my head away and sighed. When he pressed again, I said simply:

'I am worried about your death.'

Lleu laughed.

'I am worried about what I should do if you died before me.'

Lleu laughed again.

'The gods reward you for caring so much about me,' he said, 'but there is nothing to worry your pretty head about, for it is very hard to kill me.'

'Then tell me,' I begged him, 'and put me out of my misery.'

Lleu regarded me carefully. At last he said:

'If it will calm your fears, then I will.'

I smiled encouragingly.

'It would be very hard for anyone to strike me down for I can only be killed by a spear, which must be a year in the making.' He paused, still watching my face.

'And besides that, it can only be made during the times of worship on holy days.'

'Are you sure?' I asked.

'Of course! But, in fact, even with such a spear, it would still be difficult to kill me.'

'Why is that?'

'Because I cannot be killed indoors or outdoors!'

I looked at him in astonishment.

'Nor can I be killed on horseback or on foot!'

'Then how on earth can you be killed?' I asked.

'Ah!' said Lleu, 'I will tell you!'

III

IT WAS exactly a year later that I had everything ready. I had assembled it all on the bank of the Cynvael River. A bath of cool sweet water was glittering in the sun with a thatched roof overhanging half of it. Next to the bath was a buck goat tethered to a post.

When I had checked that everything was in place I went to fetch Lleu.

'I want to see if you can really stand in the way you described!' I said.

Lleu laughed and ran down to the riverbank. He stripped off his tunic and bathed in the pool. Then he stood up in the water. He placed one foot carefully on the edge of the bath and the other on the goat's back. The full sun blazed on his yellow hair as he slowly straightened up.

It was just before noon when Lleu balanced himself on the half-covered bath, and the sun was moving swiftly towards its greatest height. For an instant Lleu stood poised. And in that instant he seemed to reach into the sky. Within his body, land and water touched and in their meeting pulled a flame-shot through the air. At first I thought it was his own spear. It streaked towards him and, as the sun reached its zenith, struck him in the side. Lleu faltered but did not fall. Instead a transformation came upon him. His face twisted to a point, his eyes into hard pellets, wild hair tufted his cheeks and sprouted on his arms, his toes turned into talons, his body shrank and gathered in a feathered dart. Lleu had turned into an eagle. Then, with a great scream, the king of birds unfolded its wings and lifted up into the sky, the spear still hanging from its body.

As the huge bird disappeared into the air, Gronwy ran to me from his hiding place behind the hill and took me in his arms. His spear, crafted on holy days throughout the year, had done its magic. The lord of Penllyn had defeated Lleu and come to claim my love. As for Lleu himself, he was following his destiny.

IV

GRONWY SUBDUED the people of Ardudwy and settled into kingship. I was always at his side, my skin flushed, my eyes glowing, and a wild singing in the core of my being. For now I was with the man of my heart.

But soon enough, as I knew he would, Gwydion began looking for Lleu. His blue, magician's eyes had become worn out with staring into fire flame and probing the depths of water, searching for his boy, but seeing nothing. So Gwydion left Math's court and began to travel the land. All the time he was seeking for clues with his magician's cunning, watching out for odd occurrences.

Months passed and then we heard that Gwydion had found Lleu. Some said that the magician had taken sow-form and tracked him to the Tree of Life where Lleu hung piteously, dropping feathered flesh and worms. In an act of high magic, so we were told, Gwydion had sung him down from the tree and restored him to human form.

It was a late summer's day when Gwydion came after me. Knowing he would come, I had decided to move my maidens to the court in the mountains beyond the Cynvael river. The poor things were very frightened. They ran ahead, but kept looking back, fearing that Gwydion's magic would strike them down at any moment. In their panic, they fell into a mountain lake and drowned even before he reached them.

So when, at last, he caught up with us and the shadow of his cloak fell upon the bare mountainside, I alone remained to face him. I neither cowered nor ran from him. Instead, I lifted my head and looked at him proudly. He raised his wand, and his hair streamed out. His eyes dimmed faint blue as the sweep of the sea.

'I shall not kill you!' he said.

It was no boast. I knew he could not kill me any more than Gronwy could kill Lleu. We were fated all of us, to tread this circle until the end of time.

'I will not kill you,' he said again,' but I will do that which is worse!' But his words were empty, for we both knew I had won. I had won for I had dared to act upon my own heart's calling. I had refused to be his creation. His eyes dimmed further, his hair whipped in the wind. Now he was almost faded with the sky

'I will let you go,' his voice was curling in my ear, 'as a bird.' His voice was hard-edged.

'A bird that never sees the light of day. A bird of the dark, a creature mobbed by other birds.'

He laughed.

'Thus Flower-face shall turn into Feather-face!'

He laughed again, and his laughter poured down the mountainside. All the while he looked at me in triumph. But I laughed too. As I opened my mouth, my lips snapped into yellow and a high plaintive hoot slid through them. My fair hair splintered into brown and gold and black. My round eyes became buried in soft feathers, frilled with white. My hands were yellow, my fingers long thin points, my nails sharp curls.

Now my body was ridiculously light. I stretched out my arms, short and soft-downed as they were, and tested the currents of the air. Then I rose on their extraordinary strength and soared into the sky.

I hid for the remainder of the day and then I flew beneath the overhang of trees, hooting in the night-dark forest. All night I sat huddled on my branch. I was not looking for Gronwy. I knew where he had gone.

Gronwy had set out for Penllyn. There, from the safety of his castle, he sent messages to Lleu and offers of compensation. But I knew Gronwy's fate. So, some days later, as dawn broke, I was not surprised to see him crouching behind a standing flint beside the Cynvael river. Forced by Lleu to take a spear's blow in turn, he had begged to put a stone between himself and the blow. And now he trusted to the stone's great bulk. But, even as I watched, Lleu's streaming, flame-tailed spear seared through the stone and entered Gronwy's heart just as the first blade of sun shafted through the sky. Gronwy fell dead in an instant.

When night came again I flew into the darkness, into the cool, sweet womb of earth, seeking the sleeping time, the dreams of wisdom. My fingers delved deep into the earth, snake-wriggling below the trunks of trees. My hair became a flung green web, draping the fallen branches. My eyes were spiralling into sightless depths. Soon it would be hard to raise myself, hard to answer any summoning.

Until next springtime.

BOANN

I COME from under the mound, a daughter of the *sidhe*, the faerie people. But white foam was at my heels as I loosed their secrets on the earth.

For a time I lived with Nechtan, a lord of the *sidhe* and son of Lebraid. But Nechtan kept a secret from me, for he guarded the well of Segais. So precious was this well that only he might visit it, together with his three cupbearers, Flesc, Lam and Luam.

But I saw the eyes of each man when he had come from visiting the well – how they burst from their sockets like molten stars, streaming with inspired knowledge. And my husband, too, held secret tryst with the well, and so it was the water's dark allure that lit his eyes and touched his hair, silvering it with moonlight when he went to gaze at night, and not my own.

But I am the sacred one, fertile giver of milk and blessings, mother of the land. So why was I dishonoured, barred from the well's bright wisdom? For over all the earth, it is women who keep the waters, maidens who guard the wells and gift its life-giving waters in their golden goblets, it is women who haunt the rivers and who cast their mantles on the blue-green oceans.

Yet Nechtan claimed guardianship of the most potent well in all the land and kept me from it, while every day he gazed on it in worship.

Then one night while his eyes were bursting with so much brightness he could not even see me, I stole out in my nightshift and came to the place near the mound of the *sidhe*. I put my bare foot on the sacred land, and went fearlessly towards the waiting stillness of the well.

First I saw the fringe of hazel trees, like witch-sticks, twisted hazels, clustered round it. I felt the spongy softness of the moss beneath me, cold against my feet as I approached the twining grove of trees – the nine old wizened hags, the twisted sisters. In the places where they parted I could see the round black void. I pushed between their branches, knelt and laid my forehead on the cold stone well rim. Then I calmed my breathing, lifted up my face and saw the full moon hanging on the mirrored stillness. While I gazed, a flick of salmon's tail disturbed the surface and, at once, the shining orb blossomed and flowered in all directions. But not before I'd seen the salmon's crimson belly, how it took the hazel nut and left the husk behind it floating on the moon-flecked blackness. It was then I caught the tail-flick of a secret Knowledge stretching back through time, then flying forward, meeting itself again – the ancient pulsing power of *imbas*, the unending circle of inspired Knowing.

Then one eye burst and went dark with the revelation.

In a fever, brought by the moon-faced goddess, I snatched up the goblet lying on the rim beside me, dipped it in the water, tipped back my head and drank.

At once the liquid rushed in, spreading among my veins and sinews like molten silver. I felt its wild dance inside me, forcing me to rise. I raised my arm, my leg. I danced against the pathway of the sun, and circled three times round the well with blessings in my mouth for west and south and east and north.

And after I had danced the path three times, I heard the water boiling in its pit like brew within a cauldron. Then three great roaring waves reared up. Out they blew and burst behind me, tossing me high above the land. Caught beneath the flood-force, spinning in its rock-filled fury, I broke my hand against a stone and half my leg was wrenched away and taken. Then I broke the surface and my white breasts rose above the current, while I rode the flooding waters like a figured prow commanding where the rearing torrent carved its course.

After it had stilled its rage, the flowing river took my name, for it and I were one. And now it bites the east coast like a giant salmon, curving far into the land. But the five great fish of wisdom still lie sleek and safe within the well's black bowl, while five great singing streams run out and feed the powerful Boyne, my river.

And many come to see the well, hoping to glimpse the fabled salmon or to catch the dropping nuts of inspiration.

But others come to gaze into the Boyne, the only river that has spells of wisdom scribbled on its waters.

And I, it was, who loosed these sacred waters on the earth.

Then let each man catch at them, and every woman understand their meaning.

SABRINA

IT SEEMED to me I grew up in a tomb. A perfect concealment. My mother was treated like the goddess of a hidden spring, my father visiting her with wreaths and offerings, as though in worship.

Our home was a passaged hollow underneath the town of Trinovantum, a secret cave scoured out of the living earth and rock by soldiers on the orders of King Locrinus. The king was my father. And my mother was his subterranean bride.

And so our cave was rich – gleaming with gold and glassy crystals, fitted with thick-woven rugs and fleecy pelts. But always echoing with sighs from myriad shivering pools and silver-threaded streams.

Words are now a babble in my mouth. Locrinus – in the old tongue, loci locus, King of place, but in the new tongue 'loci, locri,' locked away, my mother and I, for her to weep and me to cry.

But why did my father keep us in a pocket in the earth? It was because he feared Corineus, the champion of the land.

Ah, Corineus! Even though he is long dead, men still speak of him in hushed tones. Corineus the brave, Corineus the bold, the Giant-slayer! For Corineus rid this land of all its giants, including the greatest of them all – the Gogmagog!

A towering twelve-foot high was Gogmagog, plucker-up of oak trees, wielder of thick-limbed trunks, shaking them like slender hazel-wands. Oh so eagerly Corineus went to meet him, with his armour stripped off. Holding out his bare arms he offered him wrestling combat, man-to-man, whereupon the giant sprang at him and wreathed his long arms, like two coiling snakes, about the Champion. Then he began to squeeze. Tighter he squeezed and tighter, until *snap*, two ribs broke on his right side, and *snap*, another on the left.

Outraged, Corineus wrestled free and, in a rush of mad and furious strength, swung the giant up onto his shoulders. Then he began to run, jogging the Gogmagog, sending his long limbs flailing. Straight towards the sea Corineus ran, and up onto a clifftop where he hurled the elongated monster down into the whirling waters. The giant fell sprawling on a reef of rocks, his body breaking in a thousand pieces, his flesh and blood sucked up by the swallowing ocean, turning its waters red before the hour of sunset.

Thus did Corineus, Champion of Loegres and of all Britain, become a great and mighty saviour, loved by all his countrymen. And yet he was my mother's fearful enemy.

This is how my mother came to fear him.

My mother was the daughter of Humber, King of the Huns. When King Humber raided the land of Alba in North Britain, Locrinus came against him and routed his army, forcing him to flee. In his flight Humber drowned beneath the waters of the river, which still bears his name.

A few days later, when the booty was delivered to Locrinus, among the gold and jewels was my mother Estrildis, a captured princess.

Locrinus used to say that the moment he saw her among the battle's bounty, he fell in love with her. For she was fairer to him than any gold or jewels. And afterwards he made this song about her:

Estrildis, like the white-throated lily in the long grasses of the hills of Loegres

Estrildis, whiter than new fallen snow
Estrildis, paler than ivory,
more precious than the spoils of bounty.
Estrildis, my quick-eyed princess,
enslaver of my captive heart.

My father offered marriage to my mother, but she was a captive foreign woman, and he was already promised to Corineus' daughter. It was too much!

When Corineus heard of it he marched to my father's court and strode into the palace, brandishing a battle-axe. *Smash!* He hit the huge Greek amphora that held the precious oil! *Smash!* He took the front legs from the long oak trestle table, setting the dishes sliding towards the flagstone floor:

'Is this how you reward the Champion of the land, the giant-slayer, the man who was the right arm of your father, Brutus? This is my lot, is it – that my daughter should be spurned, passed over for a barbarian woman? By the gods themselves, as long as I have strength in my right arm, such an insult will never go unpunished!'

Then Corineus slipped in the spilled oil and three men held him down while a fourth wrested the axe from him. Before there could be bloodshed my father's friends took him aside and urged him to honour his promise of betrothal.

And so my father married Corineus' daughter. And she ruled his palace with a spear of iron. Gwendolen, she was called, *Gwendolen*, which means 'the fair', 'the white' – but her skin was swarthy, exposed to sunlight, not like the luminous pallor of my mother, hovering like a pure-flamed ghost or spirit in the hollow of our cave.

Locrinus kept my mother hidden beneath the palace where he could come to her. And he came to her often, under guise of worship, bearing wreaths and flowers like offerings, as I said before. And it was out of their dark and secret passion I was born.

Seven years we stayed hidden in the cave, my mother and I. Then Corineus died, and straightaway my father put Gwendolen aside and brought us up into the palace where he lived with us openly. Those days were beautiful. Living in the light, walking on the green and golden earth, breathing the moving air.

But during those sun-filled months, Gwendolen, the outcast queen, travelled to Cornwall, the horned land of her father. There she rallied troops and marched against her husband. The battle was brief but fierce and at the height of it a fatal arrow found my father's heart.

After her victory, Gwendolen rose up with all the force and fury of her father and, her dark eyes flaring, ordered my mother and myself to be cast like Gogmagog, into deep and treacherous waters.

In the coiling river running between the lands of Loegres and Cymru we were thrown.

Its name, the Queen declared, from that time on would be my own.

The water is in my mouth – a thrill of bubbles escapes like a whorl of petals from the corner of my lips. Already my mother's hair is stretching long green tendrils underneath the surface, floating up like waterweed. Estrildis, Estrildis … Her limbs are dissolving, thin white spindles spreading out beneath the waving water, her eyes like glassy pebbles.

But I feel the ecstasy, the pulse and pounding of the river's flow, my own limbs stream along its paths and my hair floats out and follows. Petals, twigs and fallen leaves catch within its tumbling. Wave-wafted weeds my wedding gown, a fleece of foam my covering.

The River Goddess, I, Sabrina-Havren,
Sea-bride, Queen and Guardian of the flowing pathway.

When I gather up my robes and ride full height along my way,
my long train billows after me, flash-floods my banks –
Ah, then, men stand in awe of me!

Brutus, Corineus, Locrinus – all great men are gone,
Even Estrildis, my dear mother.
Only my name lives on:
Havren, Sabrina, Severn,
Havren, Sabrina, Severn –

And with it a woman's song.

MOTHER
GODDESSES

MOTHER

IN THE Mother aspect of the Three-fold Goddess, quite a different picture is presented. Instead of enjoying a time of wealth, fullness and general rejoicing, we find her burdened and confined. In these tales the goddess who knows herself as Sovereign is stripped of her powers. In seeking to choose her consort she is met with patriarchal prohibition and disapproval. But even if she bends to the male yoke, she undergoes the pain of living on terms other than her own. The sufferings of the goddess in these stories stem from a lack of empathy for her role as nurturer and childbearer. But her humiliation has wide-reaching consequences in terms of the land itself. When her sovereignty is disrespected not only does the goddess suffer but the land itself becomes barren.

The voice of the Mother cries for the land,
for the swell of the womb
and the milk-fed yield.

The voice of the Sovereign cries for the land,
For the swell of its fruit
And the crop in the field

The voice of the Mother cries for the land
that her child be restored
and the wounded earth healed.

DEIRDRE

Aaaaaiiiiieeeeeeeee

MY CRY swelled up, bursting from my mother's womb. The sound, strange, unearthly, scoured the rafters in my father's hall and brought the Red Branch Warriors to a standing, facing each other across the long tables, their pale hands trembling.

Cathbad held up his palms, letting his druid sleeves drift down his wrists. My mother ran to him and knelt, still quivering. He brought one hand down and laid it on her womb. I thrashed against his touch. His eyes swivelled skyward. Then he spoke:

> In the womb's dark cradling
> a woman of great beauty lies.
> It is the cry of a child,
> with wave-formed golden hair
> and eyes grey-pupilled,
> cheeks like purple foxglove,
> teeth as unspotted snow
> and lips blood red.
> Full grown, the child
> will bring on Ulster fearful slaughter,
> deaths of great and mighty warriors.
> Therefore I name her Deirdre.

While he spoke I bucked against his hands and broke my mother's waters. My birth was turbulent but short, my mother screaming in the women's quarters, my father Felim, singing loudly to his harp, trying to drown the sound and restore the mood of feasting to his hall. It must have been hard for him, trying to entertain the King and having this happen.

When the news of my birth was announced, no man raised his goblet, no Red Branch warrior clapped my father on the back, no oaths were made, no wishes of good fortune. Instead silence lay thick upon the men. It was as though I had given my *bean-sidhe* screech again.

Then the evil thought was whispered, and the whisper muttered, carried from man to man, then spoken, gathering noise until the words were shouted round the hall space:

'Kill the child! Kill it before it spills our blood!'

And then the voice I later grew to hate, calling for quiet in cat-like, careful tones. The King himself, Conchobor, raising his hand for silence, looking round the hall, easy, unafraid, a simple plan already forming in his mind – the wagering of blood for beauty:

'Slaughter,' he said, shooting the word between the edges of his teeth, 'is in our blood. Since we were boys smacking each other's hurley sticks on Emain's green, since we could weigh within our hand a long-spear, since we learned to jab and thrust and sever flesh and sinew with our knives and daggers – so we reach for these, our weapons, whenever danger threatens. Easy enough, when our enemy is flesh and blood. But … ' He paused, his fire-lit pupils holding every man's within the room, 'useless when our enemy is not. For the enemy that stalks our hall tonight is each man's fate.'

He loaded these last three words as he spoke and paused again, still holding the company with his narrowed cat's eyes.

'Yet for this we also have our training which was taught us by the druids – courage to meet our deaths, for all are timely; and wisdom to accept the bidding of the gods!'

A buzz of quiet comment rose like a cloud from the men. The king lifted his voice above it.

'So my council is this,' he said. 'Let the child alone – for the gods do not look kindly on one who slaughters infants, but, as a precaution, let her be raised apart and kept in safety. Then, when she is grown, I myself will take her to wife. And perhaps in this way I can keep her from provoking all this bloodshed. Does that seem good to you?'

The king waited while all eyes turned to Fergus mac Roth and Connall Cearnach, chiefs of the Red Branch. The two conferred together, then came forward, bowed stiffly and spoke as one:

'Your judgement seems good to us and we will be ruled by it.'

'Then I swear to you,' said Conchobor, raising his voice up to the rafters, 'by the power of Lugh who rules by day and by the Morrigan who rules by night, that if a man among you lift his hand against the child either now or when she comes of age — that man's life is forfeit!'

II

DARK WAS my second womb, a pillared hall of bones, turf-covered. All sounds of nature muffled. An empty *sidhe*-mound, an abandoned tomb. I grew up inside its silent chamber, hidden from the sight of men – from all except my tutor Cailcin, and Levacham, the druidess.

I remember how the light from the fire-pit flung shapes and shadows on Levacham's face while she spun her stories, and how I fancied in them images of fighting men, of unknown beasts, of boar or deer, of gods and druids and the people of the *sidhe*.

The *sidhe* were the faerie people, seldom seen now, but once, so Levacham told me, they had ruled all Erin. Their great God, the Dagda, had swung his huge axe and routed the race of giants, he had played his magic harp so that the seasons would come and go, and he had dined from the magic Cauldron of Plenty. The faerie race had brought the King Stone to Erin – the stone that would cry out when the rightful heir stood upon it. Their sun god, Lugh, brought the burning spear, and their first king, Nuada, the sacred sword.

Then Levacham would lay these magic symbols at the entrance to our burial mound, her long grey hair drifting about her face and her deft druid's fingers working the talismans.

I remember we had a small gold bowl to represent the cauldron. She would fill it with water and hold it up towards the sun for a blessing of the sun god. Then she had a small spearhead, sharp and perfect as an elf-blade, fashioned out of bronze. Pushed inside it was a short pole of polished ash wood. The tip of the blade was blackened by candle flame for, in our rituals, she would hold it in the heart of the wick flame until the metal turned red. She also used a stone, as high as two hand-spans, and stood it upright in imitation of the druid's circles. This she would dowse with water in our rituals, and once with blood from my hand, which she pierced with the bone-handled dagger that she used to represent the Sacred Sword.

Small as our place was, I had the freedom of the little woodland round about in which to wander. In the summer months, before the heat dried the streams, I played with the elements myself, cutting *ogham* symbols into sharpened sticks of hazel and rowan, then throwing them, like spears, across the water. And one time, I piled up stones and made a great mound, like a cromlech, big enough for a thin young girl with big dark eyes to hide in.

It was in winter that I fretted most, feeling the long nights and the blackened silence like a heavy weight upon me, as if trying to stop me growing. Then Levacham would tell me to shut my eyes while she took me travelling to the great halls of the King. One day, she said I would wander there for real. In King Conchobor's palace there were one hundred and fifty rooms, each of them three times the size of our little mound. They were built out of red oak and bordered with dimly shining copper. Conchobor's bedroom was even more splendid. The walls were clad in bronze and silver and decorated with golden birds, whose eyes, catching the morning light, glittered with rubies and diamonds. This room was large enough for thirty warriors to feast in. But it was kept only for the King and the bride that he awaited.

'How it would be to be such a bride!' said Levacham, 'with all the kingdom at your feet, with every delicacy brought to you, with every luxury that the King could command.'

Then she told me of the three great halls of the palace. The first was the Hall of the Red Branch, named for the Red Branch Warriors, the fearless champions of Ulster. In this house were kept the heads of vanquished enemies, their brains scooped out and mixed with limestone, while each empty pickled head was nailed to the wall and stared down from its place. The spoils of battle and the weapons of the dead men were also lodged here. For this was a hall of triumph. It was also the Red Branch guest-lodge.

Then there was the Royal Hall, its shingled roof upheld by nine great pillars, its windows blanked out with withy shutters, its smoke hole sucking flames and cinders from the blazing fire pit while the minstrels played and the warriors whiled away the dark nights with their feasting.

The third great hall, Levacham told me, was the Speckled House. Laid within it were the weapons of the Red Branch Warriors, cast here on the orders of the king, who forbade the carrying of weapons in the Royal Hall because of the many quarrels that broke out at feast times. And so each warrior's shield and javelin, gold-hilted sword and blue-sheened spear were housed here. Entering the hall, Levacham said, was like stepping inside a giant honeycomb, because all the burnished metal, all the wealth of decoration – the gold coils and collars on the spears, the silver scales and circles on the shields, the richly worked patterns on the cups and horns and goblets – all were touched off by the hanging lamps and threw their speckled lights upon the walls.

In the dark hollows of the night I sometimes pictured the ghoulish pickled heads hanging in silent rows about the Red Branch Hall and then I made myself think instead of bronze-bright patterns weaving cocoons of golden light around me.

As I grew older, besides my usual lessons, it seemed that every day Levacham contrived to give me some new description of the palace at Emain Macha.

'Oh, such a household that king keeps!' she said. 'They say he has as many men to serve him as there are days in the year! And as for his warriors, why they have such appetites, it is hard indeed to keep them in roasted pig and venison and vats of ale. But, as for Fergus mac Roth – he who gave his kingship to Conchobor – that man, it is said, has the appetite of seven men – in all things!'

She added this last as if in disapproval, but I never asked her why. These tales of the king's court whirling with warrior men and fiery action boiled in my mind and made my lonely life unbearable. Yet I knew I would be released in my fourteenth year, for that was when the King would wed me.

But in my thirteenth year, when I reached the borders of womanhood, I became subject to fits of feverish melancholy. All I could do was leave the mound and pace about the rough land round about. The next winter I felt so squeezed with pain, I went out into the snow with only my woollen shift to cover me. I saw a strike of dark red blood across the white-faced earth. I went towards it and saw that Cailtin had killed a deer. Then I saw the wingtip of a raven lifting as he bent towards the welling crimson. Blue-black were his ragged feathers, crouched above the redness. The bird, the drinking, and the new-dead deer, its blood steaming against the coldness, touched off flickering patterns on my inner vision. Young white skin I saw, moist crimson lips, and then a head of gleaming hair, blue-sheened.

I spent so long looking, and was so long in the fit that Levacham came searching. She found me face down in the snow, and brought me back home shivering and burning. Dreams came afterwards, of pale, pale faces. Then of one face only. Was it hanging in the Red Hall? Was it live or dead? Its lips moved wetly and its eyes shone under glossy blue-black coils of hair.

Still held by the vision I lifted from my fever and saw Levacham, her face in furrows, strain lines round her eyes. She smiled, relieved to see me waking.

But, though the weeks passed, and the fever was gone, I still languished. Nightly I was haunted by the face. Its eyes grew stronger, staring through the shining clumps of hair.

'Whose face am I seeing?' I asked Levacham. As soon as I asked I saw she knew the answer. But she shook her head with pursed lips and kept the knowledge to herself. Weeks passed and I still languished.

'I cannot live,' I said, 'unless I see him. Whose face is it?'

Then she sighed and, weighing my sickness against the king's strict orders, told me in a voice tight with resignation:

'In the King's court, famed among the Red Branch warriors for their prowess, are three close-bonded brothers.'

'What are their names?'

'They are the Sons of Usna. And tallest of the three is Naisi. It is he who has the raven-coloured hair, the white skin and the crimson lips you speak of. It is he, also who has a warrior cry of such sweet melody that it rings across the land and causes the cow to yield two-parts more milk, and any man on hearing his melodious tone, is filled with pleasure.'

As soon as she had spoken, I knew his call had come in my dreams and on the edges of my hearing. I also knew now what I had to do. I think Levacham knew it too, but it was never spoken of or plotted between us.

A few nights later, with my strength suddenly returned, I rose in the stillness of the night and thrust my tutor's spear through the far end of the mound. I pulled out sods of earth and covered the gap with hangings, then I slept. Each night I did the same, while Levacham slept soundly, until at last I made a way out through the back of the mound and through the enclosure that surrounded it. Thus I escaped my prison.

III

I SUPPOSE I might have guessed I was hidden so near the palace. It had seemed such a far-off place and so removed from my reality that I had never thought how close it must be. But with Levacham and my tutor coming and going so often, it had to be nearby. And so, not long after I had escaped and was on the forest path, I was suddenly confronted by the high walls of Emain Macha, rising like towering cliffs before me.

I looked up and saw a man standing alone on the ramparts, a strong black figure against the faint crimson of the morning sky. As the crimson turned white-bronze, the warrior lifted his two hands and cupped them round his lips. A thrilling note rang out, gentle yet rich as bird song, its sound spread until it became one with the opening day, the lifting leaves, the damply waking earth. I knew at once it was Naisi. I ran towards the palace, leaped up the high mound on my thin eager legs and passed beneath the wall where he stood.

'Fair is the young heifer that springs past me!' cried the melodious voice.

'Fair may the heifers be,' I called in reply, 'where there are no bulls.'

The warrior drew in his breath and said, this time without levity:

'Surely for you, it is the bull of the province, the king himself, who awaits you.'

I looked up at him, squinting against the brightness and seeing only a ruffled outline:

'I would choose between two bulls, and take the younger.'

'You may not so choose,' he replied, in maddeningly sweet tones, 'because of the prophecy of Cathbad.'

'Are you refusing me?' I shouted, flaring with ready anger.

'Yes, indeed, Lady.'

I did not know I had so much fire in me. I did not know that I had such resolve. All my life I had been subject to restriction. I had been reared to obedience, trained to accept the conditions of my life without question. But something had broken in me, some vision had summoned me, some call had woken me and I felt the instinctive ruling of my destiny take hold. In minutes I had scaled the battlements and now I was face to face with the milk-white skin, the raven-coloured locks, the wet, red lips. But none of these I touched. I seized his ears and held his face an inch from mine.

'Two ears of shame and mockery these will be, if you refuse me!' I shouted.

'Release me, woman!' he said, but his voice broke as he said it and I knew already the perfume of my mouth had reached him, my dark eyes and their webbed lashes had enmeshed him.

'I will not!' I answered.

Then he pulled his head from my grasp and gave a long cry, broken and discordant. All the Ulstermen heard it and sprang up, running to the Speckled House for their weapons. But first came his two brothers, the two sons of Usna, leaping to help him with nothing but their bare hands.

'What is it?' they cried. 'What has happened?

Then Naisi told them of the *geis* I had put on him. Before this day I had known nothing of this power, but now I knew it was a binding spell I had spoken and that he was obliged to honour it.

His brothers shook their heads fearfully and sadly.

'There is nothing to be done.' they said. 'Though, no doubt, evil will come of it. But for now, we will leave Ulster and go with you to another land and take her with us. No king in Ireland will refuse us hospitality.'

So that night we left with a company of one hundred and fifty warriors and one hundred and fifty women, besides dogs and servants. I had never in my life before been part of such a company.

IV

NAISI'S BROTHERS were called Ardan and Ainnli. Ardan had the same black hair as Naisi but his skin was swarthy, Ainnli had fairer hair, but the same bright lips. Neither brother was as tall as Naisi, but all three were equal in skill and deftness, and all three moved as one, especially when hunting or in combat. I learned to love all the brothers. For, although I belonged to Naisi, all three were my companions, and all three swore to protect me with their lives.

But now that we had exiled ourselves from the court we were nomads. Wandering through Ireland, the brothers offered service to one king after another, while our retinue gradually peeled away and returned to Ulster. Meanwhile King Conchobor himself gave us no respite. We never knew when he would send an ambush, or how far he would go to bribe the king who sheltered us. At last, the brothers decided we should leave Erin and take a boat across to Alba. Some of our companions left us then, watching with tears in their eyes while we lifted sail and drew away from the shores of our homeland, but the rest of our company boarded other boats and came with us.

I have wondered since if I did wrong in taking the brothers from their kinsmen, forcing them into exile with me. At the time I thought it was an adventure that would soon be ended. And the brothers encouraged me in this, telling me Conchobor would give up chasing us and that soon we would be welcomed home. Meanwhile the love between Naisi and I was so strong it shone between us and stretched out to his two brothers and even to those that accompanied us. It was like a charm or talisman that held us in its thrall.

The King of Alba was more than content to have the Sons of Usna in his country. Knowing their fleetness of foot, their skills and their combined strength was worth a whole company of regular warriors, he gladly accepted their offer of service. So the brothers stayed and built themselves three houses on the palace green. But Naisi kept me hidden in his house, fearing that sight of me might stir jealousy among the warriors and lead to bloodshed. Not for the first time did I feel my beauty was a curse upon my freedom.

And then one day when I was sitting inside the house and taking out the pieces of *fidchell*, placing them on the chequered board, ready for Noise's home-coming and our daily game, I felt a stranger's presence in the doorway. A man was looking at me with a soft gleam in his eyes. As soon as I began to walk towards him, he left without a word. But next day he came again, and called to me from the threshold, saying he had a message from the king.

'He says if you will grace his court with your presence, he will send soft cloths and drapes to furnish your house, as well as silver plates and goblets for your table.'

That night I told Naisi and his brothers what had been offered. Next day, when the man came again, I told him that my husband said we had drapes enough and cups and plates sufficient for any warrior.'

Each day the man returned with more alluring offers, each night I told the brothers, and by morning I had a courteous refusal ready. I soon learned it was the king's high-steward who came to me and who wooed me on the king's orders. But because I proved so intractable, the king began sending the brothers out into more and more dangerous battles. His plan was obvious. He wanted the Sons of Usna dead so I could be his bride.

I tried to get the brothers to move on. But they relished the testing of their prowess and met their new challenges with increasing boldness and daring. Months went by and every day I feared for them until at last I discovered there was a plot among the warriors of Alba to ambush and kill them in order to gain the king's favour.

I ran to Naisi, my face pale and my eyes puffed with weeping.

'Naisi,' I begged, 'this time you must listen to me. We have to leave this very night, because tomorrow the men are planning to kill you!'

So we left as soon as it was dark, gathering our few belongings and taking a boat to the first of the little offshore islands.

After that, we went from one island to another, still with the most faithful of our companions, living off the land and sheltering in small huts that we built as we went. The brothers were famed for their hunting skills, and boasted of being able to outrun any quarry, so we were always well fed.

I loved my life then. Our many faces round the fire at night, dining on the catch of the day. And afterwards the singing of the brothers, Ainnli's stories and Ardan's impossible riddles, and Naisi's strong arm stealing across my shoulders. This was companionship enough for me – I who had lived so long in semi-solitude. But I knew the brothers pined sometimes for the court of Conchobor, for the high walls and sturdy battlements of Emain Macha and for their fellow warriors. Yet there was such harmony between us all. If I went hunting with the brothers for the day and found myself too weary to return, between them they would carry me home on one of their upturned shields, padding its metalled surface with their soft jerkins.

Only once did Naisi make me jealous. It was while we were living on the mainland of Alba, when the Sons of Usna were still honoured guests at the king's court. One evening as they were feasting in his hall, the Lord of Duntrone's daughter turned her gaze on Naisi. When the feast was ended, she drew him to a dark corner and their lips met in a secret kiss. Afterwards he sent her a doe with a young fawn and, following these gifts, he went to visit her on his way back from fighting for the king at Inverness.

When I found out, I ceased to care whether I lived or died. I climbed into my little skiff and let it float at will on the waves. But Ardan and Ainnli came swimming after me. They caught up with the boat and turned it towards the land, pulling me home again. When he saw how distressed I was, Naisi swore three times upon his precious shield, the Luithech, and on all his other weapons, and pledged that he would never cause me such grief again – not until the day he died.

V

A FEW beautiful years we lived among the highlands and islands of Alba. Each day to me was precious, for our lives were always under threat. But through it all, the brothers never wavered in their strong belief that we would one day return to Emain Macha, pardoned and welcomed. It was only I who felt a dark foreboding. My dreams spoke to me of sly betrayals, of spilling blood, and darkness yet to come. But when I tried to tell this to the brothers, they mocked me for having a woman's fears and frailties, so I learned to keep these visions and presentments to myself.

Then one night I had a dream which was more powerful than the rest. In it I saw three birds flying strong-winged from the fortress walls of Emain towards our hut. Closer they came and closer. In their beaks they carried three small pearls of honey. These they gave us, but then they turned savage and stabbed our flesh, flying back with beads of fresh blood between their beaks.

Next day, I was sitting with Naisi inside our hut playing at *fidchell*. I remember he had just taken my knight and was waving him triumphantly in the air, when I heard a sound that lifted the hair on my arms. It was a cry far off, a warrior cry. Naisi put the carved white figure down, his ears and eyes alert like a hound that hears a master's horn.

'That is the call of a man of Erin!' he said.

'No, no!' I said at once, 'that was the call of a man of Alba.'

The call came again, closer this time, and again I insisted it was a man of Alba.

But the call came a third time and now it was close to our hut. It was the cry of a mighty warrior at the chase, a warrior coming upon its prey. It was the cry of Fergus Mac Roth, a cry well known to all the Red Branch Warriors, since Fergus was their chief.

Immediately Naisi and his brothers rushed out. There was Fergus striding towards them across the heathered hillside. He had his two sons with him, Illan the Fair and Buinni the Red and, with them, a shield-bearer to carry his famous shield, the Leochain. At once Naisi ran to him and fell on his neck, kissing him like a brother, and the warriors all embraced each other with tears of joy.

As soon as they brought Fergus and his sons into the hut, Naisi looked at me and knew by my face that I had lied to him.

'Did you know it was Fergus?' he asked.

'I knew from the first cry.'

'Then why did you hide it from me, my queen?' he asked, putting his finger underneath my chin, and tilting my face towards him.

I made some excuse and waited for the first joy of meeting to pass. Then, that night, after we had feasted, I faced the company. My voice was quiet, my eyes steady. I told them my dream and I told its meaning.

'You have a message from Conchobor offering peace,' I said to Fergus. 'But his message is nothing but the honeyed lies of a man that would play us false, a man who seeks our blood instead.'

Fergus sprang up at this, like a man wounded.

'It is not so!' he said. 'I have a message from Conchobor, it is true. But I have his promise of safe passage and, beyond that, the love and greetings of all the Red Branch Warriors who long for the return of their dear comrades.'

Then he told us of the last great feast at Emain Macha. All the nobles and knights of the household had attended so that upwards of a thousand men were seated in the Royal Hall. As he spoke, I pictured the Hall again as I had imagined it in my childhood.

Fergus' eyes burned as he told us the story:

'When all had eaten and drunk and indulged their quarrels', he said, 'the King stood up. All sounds of anger or merriment died upon his standing, while the men waited for him to speak.

'The king cried out:

'Is there anything lacking among this company tonight?'

'No, my lord,' answered the company.

'No lack in the food, I trust; no lack in the entertainment?'

'None at all, my lord.'

'Then what about the company?'

'No lack,' they said again.

The king folded his arms and spread his shoulders.

'There is a great lack in this house, and you all know it?'

Silence fell as he surveyed the waiting faces.

'It is the lack of the Sons of Usna. A pity it is indeed, that the love of a woman prevents their coming.'

Then the men murmured among themselves, as he knew they would, and all agreed this was indeed a great lack.

'If we had dared speak of it before now,' they said, 'we would have done so.'

The king smiled.

'I am not a vengeful man,' he said. 'Nor do I believe it is in the court's interest to bear grudges beyond their proper time. I therefore propose, with the permission of you all, to send ambassadors to seek out our brave brothers, to offer them pardon and to escort them home.'

Cheers rang out at his words and more jars of wine than usual were consumed that night in celebration.'

Fergus stared into the fire.

'First he asked Conall Cearnach to be ambassador,' he said 'but when he asked him what he would do if the three of you were slain while under his protection, Conall said immediately that he would slay anyone who touched them, without mercy. 'Even me?' asked Conchobor. Conall looked him in the eye and said 'Even you, my king!' Well, that put him in something of a rage, and so he turned to Cuchulainn and asked him what he would do. Cuchulainn said much the same thing so, after that, he turned to me. He was in quite a fury by then and I was worried that he might change his mind about bringing the three of you back, so I swore I would kill any Ulsterman that laid his hand against you but that I would never lift my hand against the king himself. That pacified him, and that is why he sent me.'

Fergus was smiling, believing he had played his part well. I saw his innocence, his joy at the reuniting, his guileless trust. But I also smelled the treachery of the king. I knew his purpose. I could see it laid out plain before me. But not a word of mine could sway the brothers. Nothing I said could alert them, none of my pleadings, my tears or my entreaties reached them, so great was their wish to be reunited with the men of Ulster.

And so very early next morning, with the sky still grey and the outlines of the hills still ghostly, we left our fair island. I had grieved all night. Now, as our boat drew away, I poured out my heart in sorrow:

Beautiful Alba in the east, land full of wonders.
Beloved it is to me with its bright hills and harbours,
I would never leave you were it not for Naisi.
Kilcuan, the wooded haunt of Ainnli, where I walked
with my darling by the streams and waterfalls.
And Glen Laigh, where I used to sleep beneath the rock,
feasting on fish and venison and the fat of badgers.
Glen Masan, with its white-stalked cresses of wild garlic
where we swung in sleep above the grassy harbour.
Glen Orchy, echoing with the cries of hounds,
and Naisi, lighthearted, following the chase.
Glen Etive, where my first house was raised,
fair wooded vale and milk-house of the sun.
Glen Daruel, dear valley where the cuckoo's note
sounds sweet greeting from the bending bough.
Glen Draighen, with your firm and resonant shore,
bright is the crystal water lapping on your sand,
I would never leave you were it not for love of Naisi.

VI

'I MADE two promises to the King,' said Fergus, as our boat followed the crumbled coastline of the lowlands. 'He made me swear to take you first to the house of Barach on the sea cliffs of Alba and, afterwards, not to let you stop for any meat or drink in Erin until you reached his court. The requests seemed harmless enough and, such was the mood of the king, I thought it better not to argue with him.'

Soon after he spoke, we turned the boat inland to where Barach's castle stood high and proud above the water. Barach was a kinsman of the king, and so the Sons of Usna had been careful to avoid him. But now they sprang eagerly up the path towards his feasting hall while, again, my poor heart shrank within me. I could feel it knocking out a warning against my ribs, but I forced my legs to carry me from the swaying boat up to the fortress.

Barach came out. He was a stout, broad-chested man with a look of satisfaction on his face. He welcomed us with great heartiness and told Fergus he had prepared a three-day feast to which he was invited. At this Fergus turned fiery red with shame and confusion. He spoke hotly to Barach, telling him it was an evil thing to invite him to a feast, because he must know he was bound by *geis* to accept such an invitation. He told him he had given the king his solemn oath that he would send us straight back to Emain Macha. 'How can I watch their safety, if I do not go with them?' he asked. But Barach, remaining ever courteous, refused to withdraw his invitation.

Fergus turned to Naisi.

'What shall I do?' he asked, 'You know as well as I do that to break *geis* is forbidden.' Before Naisi could reply, I said in a rush of anger:

'The choice is yours, Fergus. If you would rather abandon the Sons of Usna, who have trusted to your oath of protection, than abandon the feast, that is up to you!'

White-faced but resolved, Fergus replied: 'Although I may not leave the feast, neither will I abandon my pledge, for my two sons will accompany the Sons of Usna home on my behalf.'

At this Naisi retorted angrily:

'We do not need your sons for protection. We can protect ourselves!'

So saying, he strode out of the castle in a great rage and I and his brothers and the sons of Fergus ran out after him. Meanwhile Fergus himself sat in Barach's hall, silent and resentful, caught on the horns of the king's orders.

After Naisi's rage subsided, I took him off alone to a place where we could see down to the ocean and where the islands lay spread out beneath us. I put my arm around him and spoke softly to him.

'I have an idea,' I said. 'A plan that might help us. Why don't we sail to Rathlin Island and wait there until Fergus has finished feasting. It is still part of Alba, so we may eat and drink without breaking the king's injunction, and afterwards we can journey back with Fergus' protection.'

Naisi flinched when I spoke of Fergus' protection. His warrior blood rose in rebellion at trusting his safety to another. But I took his frowning face in my white fingers and I kissed his angry lips, and had almost persuaded him, when Ainnli and Ardan came up. Immediately all three brothers banded together, railing against the shame of cowardice, and refused to come to Rathlin. Instead, they decided to take the shortest route to Emain Macha.

That night in my despair I hardly slept, but when I did, I dreamed of darkness and blood, of Barach's smiling face and of King Conchobor himself laughing quietly in my ear. I woke moaning and told Naisi of my dreams. It seemed I was a seer now, visions were pouring past my eyes and there was no stopping or denying them. But still the brothers persisted in their blindness. Worse than that, Naisi turned on me and berated me for being a prophetess of doom.

'Your mouth speaks nothing but evil,' he said. 'and from you, my love, so incomparable in beauty.' He laughed lightly. 'Such venom coming from such lips, such utterances from so delicate a mouth – let it not fall on us, but on our enemies!'

And then he kissed me three times as if to shut my unwelcome wisdom inside me. Yet I could not stop speaking of what I saw. As we journeyed towards Erin and came to Drum Sailech, the Ridge of Willows, I cried out:

'O Naisi, see that cloud ahead of us, spreading over the palace at Emain, look how it clots with red, it speaks of bloodshed to come!'

But Naisi and his brothers laughed at my visions. At last, my hand tight upon the edge of the boat, my white face taut with foreboding, I spoke quietly and soberly to the men. I barely raised my voice, even though I knew I was speaking a prophecy:

'If when we arrive at Emain Macha we are taken into the Royal Hall of the palace, we will be safe. But if Conchobor sends us to the House of the Red Branch, then I warn you, we can expect treachery.'

This time the men gave me no answer, but something must have struck home, for it was in a grim and dreadful silence that we came at last towards the court. I, with tears running down my face, and the brothers pale now with apprehension. As I had predicted, we were conducted not to the Royal Hall where the feasting warriors would have welcomed us, but to the House of the Red Branch.

We entered that gruesome place, and saw the weapons of former enemies lying in rusting piles. As we dined, the shrunken trophy heads looked down on us in the guttering rush light and I was reminded of my nightly childhood horrors. The company we brought with us from our wanderings seemed to notice nothing awry and ate the food and drink we were served with relish. But the Sons of Usna ate little. Afterwards Naisi, looking me directly in the face, called for the king's own *fidchell* board and precious pieces to be brought to us.

Slowly he set them out, silver against gold, and began to play. Queen against queen, King against king. It was a long game. First the castles fell, and after that the men of wisdom, then, one by one, we began to lose our warriors. Holding my vanquished queen in his hand, Naisi looked at me. Fearlessly I met his gaze. And then I became aware of another's gaze. I looked up and saw at a little window high up in the wall, a man's eye peering at me. As I caught my breath, Naisi saw it too. The silver piece was still in his hand and he threw it with unerring aim. Straight as an arrow it flew and lodged in the prying eye. We heard the man scream and the clatter of a falling ladder.

We knew who it was, of course. It was the king's spy, come to tell him if I was still beautiful. We knew that because Levacham had already come to us, her old head shaking with terror. She told us she had been sent by Conchobor to report on my beauty, to see if several years of living in the wild had taken their toll upon me. She had looked at me with her wise and caring eyes and all my childhood years had rushed upon me.

'My child,' she said, 'my dear charge, even in your distress, you are still the noblest and most perfect woman in face and form throughout the land of Erin. But I will tell the king that you are wasted by your time of exile. I will tell him you are wan and thin, that your eyes are sunken in their sockets and your cheeks are fallen. Meanwhile bolt and bar the doors and defend the house until Fergus comes.'

But now we knew the king had sent another spy, a man who had climbed to the one window we had not thought of barring, and who, even now, with one eye darkened, would be running to the king to give his message.

VII

EVEN BEFORE Naisi and I had finished our game, we heard the soft scud of boots on the dry earth and the dull clank of weapons.

'It cannot be our kinsmen,' said Ainnli. 'I am sure they would not come after us.'

'These will be hired mercenaries,' said Naisi.

Then the silently creeping army suddenly gave three great alien shouts that shivered around the walls as if the hanging heads had uttered them. They ran at the doors and we heard the thumping of their spears against the beams. But the bars held against their battering. After that there was silence again, but then we heard the scrape of branches being dragged and timber piled against the walls and doorways. A noise of crackling followed, and smoky fingers began poking through the beams. Fergus' son, Buinni, leapt up and called on a company of our men to follow him. They drew back the bars and poured out of the hall. I heard the clash of shield and spear, the moan and thud of bodies falling against the walls. The troop returned quickly - or, at least, what was left of it. Now there was blood in the house, and everywhere the groans of injured men, but at least the fires had been extinguished. Buinni himself did not return. At first we thought he'd died, but one man reported seeing him, unhurt, making off towards the Royal Hall. When Illan heard of his brother's treachery, his father's battle face took hold of him.

'I will lead the next attack,' he cried, 'but I will not betray the Sons of Usna, nor my father's honour!'

So saying, he summoned a second company and, in a storm of anger, led them out against the enemy. They caught the mercenaries by surprise and cut an easy swathe through their ranks. Then they, too, returned.

After that the battle changed. I could feel it. The mercenaries were weakened by our two assaults, and the Red Branch warriors refused to come against us, so Conchobor was forced to deal his next hand.

For, now the king's own weapons came into battle, carried not by the king himself, but by his son Ficra. They were charged with power. Even from where I sat I could feel their potency. First came his two great spears, the Dart and Slaughter, then his sword, the *Gorm Glas* the Blue-green Blade, but most magic of all I felt his shield, the *Ocean*, riding towards our walls, waiting to make its dreadful utterance.

Illan had gone out again and now I could see he was pitted against the king's son. I could see them from my hiding place, fighting beside the Red Branch gate where it stood open. Illan was the stronger. He harried the prince until the loss of blood from a host of small injuries began to weaken him. Ficra faltered for a moment, and Illan seized his chance. Raising his sword above his head, he brought it down in a great arc slashing it across his chest. Immediately the *Ocean* gave the King's moan, a moan that thrummed across the land, reaching to the Three Waves where they reared around our island.

As I heard it, a new voice burst from me, strange, prophetic – the voice of a seer.

'Ah, Erin!' I cried. 'Long have I known your Three Great Waves, but never did I think their fearful roaring would come against the Sons of Usna!

O, Wave of Truth, loud-tongued in the mouth of the Bann in Derry, how could you fail to see such treachery!

O Wave of Rury, rolling the tide at Dundrum, how could you raise your voice against such warriors!

O Wave of Cliodna, riding white-robed along the Glendore Harbour, how could you cry against such dear companions!'

In the mist that flooded my sight in the Red Branch Hall, I heard the moan of the king's shield. In my mind's eye, I saw it touch each of the Three Waves on the island's shores. But also in my seeing was a man sitting beside his dun. The hair massed about his head was yellow as a stack of hay, his right arm was stout with muscles – as well it might be, for the sword in his hand was triple edged. Beside him lay a crimson shield with rivets of white bronze. I knew who it was – Conall Cearnach, son of Amergin, fellow Red Branch chief and friend of Fergus. The shield that lay beside him was the Lam-tapaid.

I had heard it said that so fleet of foot was Conall that if a fort of seven gates was ambushed, he would be found at every gateway. And now from where he sat Conall heard the *Ocean's* great moan and the roar of answer from the Wave of Truth. As soon as he heard it, Conall sprang up and ran towards Emain, eager to defend the king he thought was dying.

Illan and Ficra were still in combat, but Illan's sword was pressed to Ficra's neck when Conall suddenly appeared beside them. Conall raised his triple-sharp sword and struck through Illan's helmet, biting deep into his head. From my hiding place I saw the son of Fergus fall, his gold hair welling crimson. As the life left him, he cried out:

'O Conall, fateful and terrible is the blow struck in haste and fury! For you have killed the son of Fergus, who was defending the Sons of Usna!'

Then Conall, heartstruck with grief and fury, seeing the death gleam stealing over Illan's face, whirled round and swung his sword at Ficra, slicing through his neck. I saw Ficra's headless body fall and Illan, raising himself in one last effort, throw his weapons into the Red

Branch House. Then he seized the *Gorm Glas* out of Ficra's lifeless hand and fell face down upon it.

As I sat on, frozen to my place, I saw how the battle fared. Hour upon hour the bodies thudded to the ground outside our prison hall, as many – men said later, as the stars in heaven. It was chiefly Naisi and his two brothers who despatched them. Many were among our company and many more joined our side. But always it seemed the king could call up fresh supplies of hirelings. More fires were lit against our walls and Arden led a troop to put them out. Then Naisi, coming back from a great and bloody rout, saw Levacham watching with a pale face and called to her to climb up onto the ramparts and look out across the plain for Fergus' army. The druidess hurried off but came back shaking her head, saying she could see nothing but the open plain and cattle browsing.

With no hope of Fergus' help, and knowing they could not hold out much longer, Naisi and his brothers decided to break out from the Hall and take me to a place of safety.

Naisi led me from my place and put me in the middle of the hall. Then all the men stood round and hid me with their bodies, making a fence of shields and bristling spears. In early dawn we opened the great doors of the Hall, marched out and cut through the hirelings in our tight-formed ranks. Our escape was well planned and easy. Too easy. As we went out of Emain Macha my heart lifted for a moment. But the seer in me knew a curse was on us. If the Sons of Usna could not be overcome by fighting, then the king would use druid magic.

Soon afterwards, as I had guessed, the wily Conchobor called on the druid Cathbad to help him. Cathbad, who was his natural father. Cathbad, who served the cause of Ulster. Cathbad, who thought he could trust his son.

'Stop them,' begged the king. 'Stop them so that I can bring them back to Emain and have them sit in honour among my warriors again.'

And so it was that, as we marched swiftly out of Ulster in close formation, all around us rose a sea so thick and sticky it seemed as if we were steeped in honey. As it climbed up our bodies, the warriors threw down their weapons and spread their limbs trying to swim as best they could. But the powerful liquid held us like struggling insects. As it disappeared again, we saw Conchobor's soldiers picking up our weapons. They closed in and formed a circle around us. And, because we were now unarmed and defenceless, they captured us with ease and led us back into Emain Macha.

There on the green before the palace, Conchobor commanded the three Sons to stand as one before him.

'Who will sever their heads for me?' he cried

Only my screams cut the silence. No man stirred. No Red Branch warrior would come forward.

'Who will it be?' came Conchobor's call again. But no man answered.

'Who will do this for me?' called the king once more.

This time Maini of the Rough Hand shuffled forward. He had lost his father and two brothers in the battle. Conchobor handed him his sword.

'I am the youngest!' It was Ardan's young voice ringing out. 'Slay me first, so that I may not see the deaths of my poor brothers!'

'No slay me, first!' cried Ainnli.

But Naisi, his black hair billowing about his shoulders, raised his hand:

'The sword that Manannan gave me can cut cleanly. One blow will take our three heads from our bodies so that we can die together.'

None of the brothers flinched as the sword was brought and raised by the warrior Maini. But Naisi lifted his eyes and held me with his gaze until his head dropped.

After they fell, a cry went up from all the Red Branch Warriors. Three shouts of grief they sent out, echoing round the walls of Emain,

three shouts rising to the heavens, three cries of sorrow for the
Sons of Usna.

VIII

Three headless bodies lie on the palace green. Beside them three pale
heads with staring eyes.

  Now I alone kneel on the blood-drenched sward beside the
brothers. I alone kiss the headless body of my Naisi.

*Ochone! Ochone! Blood is before my eyes. The heads are speaking, drained
of all colour.*

  *Lips blood wet and blue hair gleaming, six eyes dull, and yet still
looking. Nailed they will be soon, among the hanging ones, the enemies of
Ulster. Waking and sleeping – how they will haunt me now!*

My mouth is on his neck. Blood in my throat.

'A Curse on the King!' – *but it is not my voice, blood-stopped.*
I hear the old seer, Cathbad, screaming:

'Never a catching sea I'd make with willing. Never a sea to trap the
brothers. Only a sea to bring them home for pardon. A curse on the
king for druid's eyes deceiving!'

My torn hair is hanging from my fingers. How did it come here?
'Naisi, Naisi!'

'A curse upon the house! A curse upon the sons! A curse!'

Three Lions of the Hill are dead!

Now I alone. Alone, I. Weep.
'A Curse on the House of Emain.
For Conchobor has broke his word!'

Three Falcons. King's Sons.
Three Great Warriors. Flowers of Ulster. Gone.
Grief. Bitter, bitter in their going.

'A Curse on the Land of Ulster for its king's deceiving!'

Three Sons gone!
So forceful and strong
But to me, so gentle.
Now there is no hearing in you, Naisi,
For your Love's lament.

'A Curse on the sons, a curse on the line of Conchobor, my seed!'

The day, long, dark.
No living now is left me.

'Thrice-cursed, thrice-cursed, the king! A son of mine no longer!'

Grave-gazing, deadly illness numbs me.
Heart-stopped. No more life without the love of Noise.
Dig the grave wider.
Three heads, three bodies and a fourth –
my own, blood-covered. Cover us with stones.
Mark out the place.
Spell it in bitter letters etched in ogham:

The Sword of Sorrow
cuts the heart so deep.

BRANWEN

I am the whiteness of silence.
The voice of the silence, the whiteness.
Before time I was the cold white earth.
I am the white raven of the strong eyes that flies by itself.
I am the white bird of rebirth, the milk of the young heifer calf,
I am the first light, the void of calm between day and night,
the hollow whiteness beyond time.

I AM named Branwen meaning 'the white raven.' But men, being men, preferred to call me Bronwen the 'white-bosomed'. Perhaps they thought my breasts were the last comfort, the last soft press of beauty in a world gone mad.

My brother Bran, 'the raven', was a giant. No house could contain him. He lived in the great outdoors and *was* the great outdoors. The roots of him were in the bones of the land – the shaggy forest was his hair, the harsh boulder his fist, the knuckle of hill his shoulder. I loved him and I trusted him. When I was a child he had protected me, lifted me in his arms, and shielded me from my brother Efnisien's blows. Efnisien was my half-brother, a canny vicious child, twinned with Nisien. And because Nisien was too gentle to fight with him and Bran was too big, Efnisien tried to fight with me instead.

And then there was Manawydan my other brother. Manawydan – the mysterious boy, the quiet young man who kept his own counsel.

I was the only woman in the royal household so I had the ancient title. I was a Matriarch of Britain, one of the Three Great

Matriarchs. I grew up knowing this, and much was made of it. Yet it seemed an inheritance in name only, for it was always Bran who carried the power in our family, which was why, after we grew up, it was Bran who became king. I loved him with a blind love, a love that never saw how much he took from us, how much he had already taken from me. And if Nisien saw, he kept peace about it, and if Manawydan saw, he kept it to himself. But it seems to me now that Efnisien saw it all and burned with fury.

Then came the fateful day. My brothers were all sitting on the rock of Harlech, Bran like a great tree arching over the others. Below them the grey sea heaved and spattered against the rock. When they looked far out there was nothing to be seen on the horizon. Even the spectral tracings of the coast of Erin lay in shroud.

Nisien and Efnisien sat together as usual, and Manawydan a little apart. Yet as they looked, they saw what seemed at first a speckling on the water, like a handful of nuts floating out from the shrouded land. Gradually the nuts grew in size until, before my brothers' eyes, they began sprouting masts and sails. Soon enough the men were able to make out thirteen ships heading towards our coast. The fleet of vessels was magnificent, each ship flying a flag of rich-coloured satin. Flames of crimson, tongues of peacock blue, plumes of magenta flickered tantalizingly upon the rigging like a company of dancing women flaunting themselves before the king.

One of the ships pulled ahead of the rest and, as it came near, there was a flash of silver as a shield was raised, point upwards, in the sign of peace. Then boats were put down from the ships and a convoy of men began rowing into land.

From his place on the rock, Bran hailed the fleet.

'May the gods be with you!' he boomed. 'Welcome to my kingdom!'

The ships sailed closer.

'Whose fleet are you,' Bran called again. 'Who is your leader?'

The upturned shield caught the light once more and shivered like a tear about to drop. A weak voice shouted out a greeting. But it was still too far away to hear.

The boats came closer.

When they reached our coast, a chorus of voices shouted:

'King Matholwch of Erin is here and these are his ships.'

'Then let him come ashore,' said Bran.

There was silence while the pennants fluttered, flirting with the sky, the sea, the land.

'He will not set foot on your shore unless you grant his request.'

It was one voice now, more distinct.

'What is that?'

'He wishes for the hand of Branwen in marriage and to make an alliance of the two islands.'

Perhaps Bran paused at this. I like to think so. But, if so, it was only for a moment.

Then he spoke for me and his loud voice travelled across the bay.

'Bring him ashore so that we can discuss the matter.'

And once he had said these words, there was no going back.

And so King Matholwch came ashore. His clothes were as fine as the pennants waving on his ships, his step was light, his mouth seemed always open in a smile. Although it was such short notice, a hearty feast was hurriedly prepared, and honours showered upon the king of Erin and his retinue.

Early next day Bran summoned his council. It was a council of men, all elders of the land. I was not present. But I know they debated my fate. Bran told me afterwards with pride how they said I was a national treasure and the most beautiful woman in the world. They regretted losing me, but in the end they decided to give me to Matholwch in order to keep the peace between the lands. More than this, they hoped such a gifting would finally unite the islands. All this was decided in my absence. Nisien was there, and Manawydan. Only Efnisien knew nothing of the plan, being away on other business.

And perhaps because Efnisien would soon be home, the thing was done in haste. Both parties set out for Aberffraw, a place on the estuary. Our people processed there on land while the company from Erin sailed along the coast in their ships. Tents were set up there, because Bran was too huge to be housed. And this time an even greater feast was prepared. A bridal feast.

Bran himself presided over the feast. Manawydan was sitting on one side of him and Matholwch on the other. I was placed next to Matholwch. I remember he smiled at me as I sat down beside him and, bowing his head slightly, raised his goblet to me.

Long into the night we feasted. As the hours passed, slowly my husband's eyes became blurred, but there was still a light that fluttered in them when he looked at me. Grease was round his mouth from the bones of ox and deer when he suddenly lunged towards me, and kissed me on the lips. His hand squeezed my waist. He laughed and all the company laughed with him.

'Well, my Beauty,' he said, breathing hard and pushing against the table to stand up. 'It's time to find our quarters!'

His men roared approval and, at a sign from Bran, our company roared too.

Then Matholwch took my hand and, staggering a little, led me to the fine pavilion that had been prepared for us.

It was in the depths of the night, while the marital celebrations were still in force, that Efnisien finally arrived. He climbed down from his horse and called a groom. Then he heard the sound of blowing breath and brittle clinking coming from the makeshift stables.

'Whose horses are those?' he asked the groom sharply.

'The horses of King Matholwch of Erin,' replied the groom.

'What are they doing here?' asked Efnisien.

'Why, the King himself is here and even now is sleeping with your sister Branwen. They are man and wife.' the man answered.

'Have they given away so excellent a woman as my sister without my consent!' shouted Efnisien, the blood coming to his head. 'Such an insult is intolerable!'

Efnisien's temper had always been hot, but now he was beside himself with rage. The thudding of hooves was in his ears, his skin burned red, a force pushed through him like the hero spasm of Cuchulainn. In the heat of the moment he drew his sword and rushed upon the horses. As Matholwch lunged at me in his drunkenness, pulling roughly at my clothes, Efnisien tore blindly at the horses, cutting their lips and slicing off their ears, lopping their tails, disfiguring their rumps. As he defiled the horses, so the foreign king defiled the white mare of the land, heaving himself upon me, stopping my mouth, and thrusting himself within me in an act of blind possession.

At first light next morning the horses of Erin were found savaged and bleeding.

II

I WOKE alone in our pavilion. Outside I heard the sound of Matholwch's outraged voice:

'If they intended to do me such gross insult, why did they give me the woman, their chief treasure?'

He was answered by the muttered voices of the men, and then I heard the sounds of fast movement and the gathering of possessions. By the time I came out of the tent they were halfway to their ships.

I sent a messenger running to Bran with the news. Straightaway he sent Iddig and Hefeyd the Tall after the king. They ran to the shore and stopped him just before he reached the ships.

'Why you are leaving so hurriedly?' asked Iddig.

'By all the gods!' replied Matholwch, 'if I had known how I would be treated, I would never have come here in the first place!' Then he told the two men about the maiming of his horses.

'But I cannot understand how you would do such a thing after giving me so excellent a girl as Branwen.' he said.

'For our part,' said the messengers, 'we swear it was not the desire of anyone at court to insult you in such a way. Indeed, Bran will be even more horrified by this than you are.'

'That may be so,' answered Matholwch. 'Nevertheless, he cannot take back such an insult.'

The two messengers ran back to Bran and reported what the king had said.

'We must stop him,' said Bran. 'For the sake of peace between our two countries, we cannot let him go back angry like this.'

Then he sent my brother Manawydan with Hefeyd the Tall and Unig Strong-shoulder, with offers of reparation.

The men caught up with Matholwch as he was boarding his ship. They hailed him and requested that he would wait a while and listen to Bran's offer. With a curt nod of the head, the king left the ship and came towards them.

'Bran sends words of greeting and says he is willing to make good this insult to the High King of Erin,' said Manawydan.

'Bran offers to replace every maimed horse with one that is sound. Moreover he offers as honour-price a staff of silver as thick as the little finger of the High King of Erin, and as tall as the High King. He also offers a plate of gold, round as the sun itself and wide as the High King's gracious countenance.

Added to this, Bran wishes me to say that the insult against the High King was done against his will and without his knowledge or consent. The insult was carried out by his half-brother, a member of the royal household. Because of this he wishes the High King to understand that it would be difficult to have the man put to death. But if the High

King will agree to come and meet Bran face to face, then he will make peace with him on whatever terms the High King desires.'

Matholwch listened to all this in silence, tilting his head and observing the men warily. When they had finished he said tersely:

'Very well, I will hold counsel with my men.' Then he waived them away.

While Bran's men waited at a distance, Matholwch and the men of Erin sat together on the banks of the estuary and considered Bran's offers.

'If we reject these terms,' said one of his advisers, 'might we receive a greater offer?'

'On the contrary', said another, 'it is more likely we shall receive a greater insult.'

Matholwch drew his heavy cloak about him.

'As it stands, I have been offered terms that I may name myself,' he said. 'Let us return and see what greater reparation might yet be had.'

So the king and his retinue returned to Bran's court.

That night the tables for feasting were laid out beneath silk tents draped with precious hangings as before. Again Bran sat in his place with Matholwch on his right hand and Manawydan on his left. I sat beside the king of Erin. But, perhaps because I was now his wife, he barely looked at me.

Bran began conversing with Matholwch, but it was like speaking into a dry well, for the king's face was smooth as bronze and he spat out answers like small stones from between his teeth.

I could see what was going through Bran's mind. He was remembering the fair speech, the studied courtesy and ready humour of the king, how only the previous day he had laughed and slapped his thigh at every joke, and how he had pulled out glittering stories and riddles from his stock and entertained the host with a stream of lively talk. Now Bran was thinking that the man was discontented with the offer and that he would have to make a greater one. He was also thinking about me – that I was a woman despoiled, unfit for any other king. Whatever the price, I knew Bran would make sure I was taken to Erin as Matholwch's wife. What I had not guessed was how far he would go, or what he was prepared to offer.

After a while Bran gave up trying to converse with Matholwch. He looked him in the eye and exclaimed:

'Why man, you are nothing like the companion of the other night! For then your voice rang with warmth and goodwill. But if the change in you is because you consider my offer too low, then I will increase it as much as you want.'

'May the gods look well on you,' said Matholwch.

Perhaps my brother had taken too much wine, or perhaps he thought petty bargaining was beneath him. He looked again into the young king's eyes.

'I will greatly increase your compensation,' he said, 'I will give you a cauldron of great magic that has this property: whenever a man is killed, if he is thrown into its bowl, he will rise whole again the next day – whole, that is, except for the power of speech which will be taken from him.'

I saw a flicker of recognition pass like a tongue across Matholwch's face.

'Your offer is most generous,' he said, 'and we accept.'

And now the king was changed. His face became alive. He noted every joke and comment made by Bran. He kissed my hand and praised my brown-gold hair, paid tribute to my soft white breasts, my flawless skin, my olive eyes. 'Like two floating boats', he said, 'deep enough for a man to sail away in.'

He signalled for his goblet to be filled again.

'Oh Branwen,' he breathed, and fumes of heavy wine lay on his lips, 'you are a fair catch indeed!'

But the colour was rising in my cheeks, and it was not for his fondling of my thigh beneath the table. I was thinking of the cauldron.

III

ALL THROUGH my childhood I had heard stories of the cauldron. To me then it was just a magical idea. I knew it was a vessel of plenty and that it fed the living and revived the dead. I also knew that, in earlier times, the goddess Ceridwen had brewed within it the great potion of the *awen*.

I was told that it was lost for a time but that now it lay under the sea, held in the glaze of the waters. It had no form of its own, but was shaped by the breath of nine maidens kneeling in a circle and making incantation. I knew that it was iridescent, that its rim was strung with pearls, which lay upon it like a ring of gleaming moon-white teeth. I saw it in my mind's eye dim and indistinct, swirled and gaping like a huge and swallowing mouth, a beckoning womb.

Although it haunted my imagination throughout my childhood, never in my wildest dreams did I think that I would actually see it.

Then one day, after Bran became king, we were all looking out from the rock of Harlech when we saw a vessel coming towards our shore. It was riding dangerously low in the water. When it reached the shallows, two armed warriors climbed out and dragged it up the beach. Then they climbed up the cliff and made their way to our court. The two warriors were huge, almost as huge as Bran himself, and, as they came nearer, we saw that they were man and wife. As soon as they reached the court the man took off his helmet and his yellow hair fell down his back. We saw then how fearful he looked. His face was scarred and blistered and one eye gleamed black under a turf of eyebrow. But the woman was even bigger than the man, and her face and hands were also scarred with livid burn marks. Besides that, her belly was greatly distended, as if she had swallowed a monstrous child.

The extraordinary couple said they had a huge cauldron with them, and that it was lying in the boat. They told us they had come from Erin and had fled to our shore because their lives were in danger. They begged Bran to give them protection and, in return, they offered him the cauldron, which, they said, had wondrous powers.

'What powers are those?' Bran asked.

'My lord', said the crag-faced giant, 'the woman standing here before you carries in her belly a man growing to full size, who will very soon be born. In fact, every six weeks a fully armoured warrior springs from her womb. Yet it is not her own doing, but the power of the cauldron that gives her this ability.

At his words all those within the court quailed, appalled by the thought of an ever-growing giant army. Only Bran was not intimidated, being of a size with the fearsome couple. He welcomed them to the kingdom and courteously accepted the gift of the powerful cauldron. As for the huge warriors that sprang from the woman, Bran made an army of them and trained them to defend the island.

We kept the cauldron in the palace. It was made of iron. There were no pearls round the rim. It was huge and plain, its belly was a vast cavern stained with black for, like the giants themselves, it had escaped a terrible fire. The couple told us the cauldron's greatest power was manifested during wartime. They said that when dead warriors were thrown into it and the cauldron was heated on a fire, the men would be revived to fight again.

At that time I found it hard to believe all this, for the cauldron seemed too dull to ring with any power or inspiration. In my heart I mourned the cauldron of my childhood's fancy – the bright vessel formed of songs and dreaming, the incandescent bowl that fed the spirit, the bowl in which Ceridwen brewed the potion of poetic wisdom. But I tried to put the two vessels together – the real one and the one of my imagining, and find a blending of their powers. So I made a song about it.

Beneath the dark waters
was I made. Nine
maidens shaped me
with their breathing,
weaving my pearl-rich
brim and preparing
my potent brew,
my *awen*
of initiation ...

I come from a time
of Ancient Knowing.
Giants took me,
I gave abundance,
food and offspring.
Succour is found in me,
regeneration; dumbstruck
warriors spring from me,
well versed in battle.

I am the Womb of Making,
succouring the living,
brewing life's bright
elixir and the baleful
poison. Reviver
of the dead, bestower
of *awen*: wisdom,
knowledge, threefold
inspiration.

When I sang my song I felt as if I was the cauldron, my belly
shining with its *awen* and a bright child waiting to be born within me.

IV

NEXT DAY Bran gave Matholwch the horses as agreed and, because there were not enough tame horses to make up the number and fulfil the bargain, Bran gave him several colts as well.

That night the two kings feasted together once more and our two courts with them.

When he was sufficiently charged with wine, Matholwch turned to Bran.

'Where did the cauldron come from,' he asked, 'the one you have just given me?'

'It was given to me by a man who came from your land,' answered Bran, 'and for all I know, the cauldron itself was found there too.'

'Who brought it?' asked Matholwch.

'Llassar Llaes Byngwyd,' said Bran. 'He came here with his wife after their escape from near death in a fire.'

Bran turned towards Matholwch.

'And I shall be surprised indeed if you yourself know nothing about it,' he added meaningfully.

There was an uncomfortable pause. I sensed my husband struggling with his pride. At last he said reluctantly:

'I do know, my lord, and I shall tell you as much as I know.'

Then he began to relate the story and, despite his reluctance, his blood was soon fired by the task of telling.

'It was when I was out hunting in Erin one day that the strange adventure occurred,' he said. 'I was in a forest on top of a mound that overlooks a large lake, and you will understand soon enough how it came to be called the Lake of the Cauldron for, as I looked down, I saw a great disturbance in the waters. And after that, I saw a marvellous sight – a huge man emerging from the lake. He had yellow hair flowing down his shoulders and an enormous cauldron on his back. He was a giant of a man – the very dark lord himself, I thought to myself, or else a fearful monster. There was a look about him, which even from my perch upon the hill, I could tell was crooked and devious. Well then, he came towards the bank and then, wonder of wonders, I saw that behind him, rising also out of the waters, was a woman. But, upon my soul, the woman was even bigger than the man! As I looked down in astonishment, there she was, striding across the lake, her overloaded belly floating out before her. The monstrous couple came steadily towards the hill and, looking up, saw me astride my horse and hailed me with loud and deafening voices. I had my retinue about me so I hailed them back and invited them up for audience.'

While Matholwch had been telling his tale, the hum of conversation had slowly died within the tent. By now all eyes were fixed on him, all ears alert to hear his story. Aware of this, Matholwch shifted in his chair, and cleared his throat loudly before resuming his tale.

'I remember how the cauldron clanged on the man's back as they climbed the hill,' he said. 'They set it down in front of me and told me that the woman could conceive a full-armed warrior every six weeks. It seemed that in some way her powers were connected with the cauldron.'

Matholwch paused again for effect. He stretched out his leg and touched my foot.

'Well, of course, I wanted the cauldron,' he said. 'But I could have done without the giant couple. Nevertheless, I think I may say that I was courteous enough. I offered to maintain them and I kept them for a year.'

He gave me a sly wink.

'I cannot begin to tell you how much they cost me in food and liquor,' he said. 'And as for those infernal full-grown warrior children, I heard soon enough that they were running wild and harassing my people.'

His eyes darted around the company.

'So much so in fact that, by the second year, my people threatened to rise against me unless I rid them of these monstrous pests!'

Matholwch spread his hands.

'So what could I do? Well, of course, I called my council to debate the matter. We knew the giants would never go of their own accord and, because of their fighting skills, we knew we couldn't possibly overcome them.'

He looked around the table. Every face was bent upon him.

'So we made a plan. We decided to build an iron chamber. The thing was vast. Quite a feat of forging, in fact, and the final touch required the cooperation of every smith in the land. Messengers went out to every one of them, and they came in by night and gathered round the chamber brandishing their hammers and tongs. By that time, inside the chamber we had the giant and his wife with all their family. We had already invited them to a feast. We made much of this, saying it was a house built specially in their honour. The first house in which they had ever been able to stand up.'

He laughed sneeringly.

'Of course, the poor fools were deeply flattered. They sat at a huge table with all their sons around them and began to eat. And all the time my men were passing round the strongest wine and ale, my minstrels were playing loudly on their pipes and singing raucous drinking songs, while outside my smiths were piling charcoal all around the chamber. Round went the ale again, and the songs became louder. After a time, their wits being fuddled, the outsized family failed to notice the servants slipping away and the entertainers disappearing one by one. Meanwhile the smiths worked quickly. They set fire to the charcoal and fanned the flames with bellows. Thus the first thing those monsters noticed was an overpowering heat. Most were too drunk by then to move. But outside the chamber the smiths were working harder, blowing fiercely with the bellows, firing the walls until they had them blood red with heat.'

Matholwch bent to his food again.

'So how did they escape?' asked Manawydan.

Matholwch finished his mouthful slowly and put down his glass.

'It seems that the parents were not as drunk as we had anticipated,' he said. 'In fact they tried to hold some sort of council inside the chamber.'

He reached for an ox bone.

'Quite intelligent really,' he said, picking at the flesh. 'Surprising in the circumstances. Do you know what their plan was? To wait for the heat to make the walls white and then try to break through them and escape. And so they huddled together in the middle of the chamber and waited, willing themselves to withstand the heat – which, by then, I can tell you was almost overpowering. They waited while the walls glowed red, they waited while patches of white appeared, they waited until the whole place thinned and became like the inside of a shell. Then Llassar Laes whatever-his-name-is ran at the wall and shoved his shoulder right through it. After he had made the breach he kept on running, and the hideous wife was right behind him, wearing the cauldron over her belly for protection. As soon as the two of them were through, the molten edges of the wall caved in and twisted together. This was too much for the rest of them. Most of them had passed out with the heat or the wine by then anyway. So in the end not one of them escaped.'

Matholwch ended the story with a grin of satisfaction.

'And that is how we rid ourselves of the pestilent army,' he said with finality. 'But the parent couple got out with the cauldron.'

He turned to Bran.

'And I expect that is when they came to you,' he said.

'It is indeed,' said Bran quietly, 'and they bear the scars of their ordeal to this day.'

'Then how on earth are you controlling all those hideous warriors?' asked Matholwch, 'for I presume the woman is still producing them in droves!'

'As to that,' answered Bran, 'I use them to my advantage. I quarter them throughout the land and use them to defend the coasts and boundaries. They are a splendid fighting force. I sometimes wonder what I'd do without them.'

There was silence at the table while Matholwch shifted in his chair.

'Well, for all that,' he said, 'I am glad indeed to have the cauldron returned to me. And without its fearful owners!'

His men laughed appreciatively, and the pipers and harpers took up their melody again.

Next morning we set sail for Erin carrying the cauldron with us.

V

THE FIRST year I was in Erin I took its people to my heart. I had brought numerous gifts and riches with me from the Island of the Mighty – jewelled rings, fine brooches and other royal gems. All these I bestowed on the lords and nobles of Erin and soon I became honoured throughout the land. I flourished at that time and felt that I could count many of its people as my friends. Before the year was out my belly began to swell like the waiting cauldron, and in the second year I gave birth to the bright child of my dreaming.

This event was greeted with much feasting and celebration. The boy was named Gwern, meaning 'alder'. 'Gwern son of Matholwch' was the phrase on everyone's lips. And, of course, my boy child stole my heart. Every day was a wonder to me. Through his baby eyes I saw the world anew, and with him I discovered again each gem of nature. So it was bitter indeed to have to give him up for fostering when he was barely old enough to walk. But it was the custom amongst kings and nobles. So Gwern was sent to the best house for boys in Erin, and with that I had to be content.

But I grieved his going and could have done with the comfort of friendship. Yet soon after he'd gone I noticed a change come over my people. There was a sudden coldness in their manner towards me, an unspoken resentment. I was shown less honour, treated with less respect. I asked Matholwch about it, but he ridiculed my worries.

Nevertheless, after a while, even he began to draw away from me. At the same time, rumours of uprisings reached him and he became distracted. Whenever I saw him his brows were pulled together with anxiety. On one occasion I heard him shouting something at the council meeting, but when I asked him afterwards if there was something wrong, he turned on me brusquely and said I was mistaken.

Then one black day the mounting resentment came to a head. Matholwch called me into the long room where he was holding council. The face he turned on me was one of anger mixed with fear.

'Now,' he thundered at his men, 'I am tired of hearing about these stirrings and uprisings up and down the country! If, as you say, the maiming of our horses still rankles in all your hearts, what would you have me do? Do you really want my wife to bear the punishment for this old insult?'

He stepped towards me, but kept his eyes on the men.

'Is this what you want me to do?' he shouted at them. Then he struck me in the face.

I fell to the floor in all my finery. No man of the council helped me up.

While I lay there Matholwch loomed over me.

'You shall take punishment for the insult of your people,' he thundered. 'From now on you shall serve us. Your place will be in the kitchen, preparing food!'

Then he waved a hand and two servants came running in. They lifted me abruptly from the floor and carried me down to the kitchens. My robes were stripped from my back and I was dressed instead in the clothes of a kitchen maid. I was immediately set to work on the preparation of food for the daily feast – a feast such as I myself had presided over every day of my life. But my humiliation was still not complete. When the day drew to an end, the butcher entered the kitchen with his hands still bloodied from cutting up raw meat. He came over to me and boxed my ears, leaving blood marks on my neck. With my head still ringing with the blow, I heard him tell me curtly that he was just following his orders.

From that terrible day onwards, I was forced to work continually in the kitchens. All day I worked to prepare the food, and every night I endured the same boxing of my ears. I was banished from my own chamber and slept instead in a small dark room in the basement of the palace.

I made no friends in my time of insult. I think the servants pitied me, but they were unable to treat me as one of them. I was branded with the mark of my home country, the Island of the Mighty – a land now thought of with scorn and derision. At first I hoped some trader would hear of my suffering and take the news to Bran, but then I was told that the seaways were closed. No ships, coracles or ferryboats were allowed to sail to my country, and any men that landed here from its shores were imprisoned so that they could not return.

Three long years I endured this treatment. Throughout that time I was shunned and treated like an outcast. I worked as a servant by day and cried myself to sleep every night. But even in my sleep I found no refuge. Throughout the night my mind was plagued with wild and fevered dreams. Sometimes I saw Matholwch raising his arm against me, then I would see his face dissolving, turning slowly into Bran, his long arm reaching almost to the sky. And then I would see Bran turn to me, his eyes like flints, and send me across the waters over and over again, each time bartering my maidenhood anew. At other times I dreamed the iron cauldron thundered after me, its great mouth gaping, seeking to engulf me. After such dreams I woke shivering, and tried to conjure in my mind the beautiful breath-wreathed Bowl of Making, gleaming with pearls and guarded by nine spirit-women. Had there ever been such a cauldron, I wondered in my despair.

Then one day as I was kneading pastry, out of the corner of my eye I saw an iridescent flash of blue-green feathers land on the corner of the kneading trough. It swayed for a moment, one wing extended, and I saw it was a starling. I put out crumbs and every day after that it fluttered to my trough, hopeful for more. I began to tame it, stroking its breast and the pink patch beneath its beak. As the months passed, I taught it to open its beak like a yellow trumpet and form new sounds. Little by little I taught it my words of suffering and after three years were up I thought it had learned enough. Besides that I could wait no more. I wrote of my humiliation in a letter to Bran and, rolling the tiny parchment tightly, attached it to the root of my starling's wing. Then I sent the little bird across the waters to my brother's court.

VI

SEVERAL WEEKS went by. Then one morning Matholwch's servants came to fetch me. They brought me up from the kitchens and marched me into the Great Hall. I stood before all the court dressed in my cap and servant's clothes, with flour still sticking in my hair and hands. As I fought to retain my dignity, one of the messengers addressed me:

'Lady, ' he said, 'we have heard a report of strange sightings coming from your land.'

I stood in silence.

'We have heard that there is a dense mass of trees advancing towards our country across the waters. Beside them is something that looks like a mountain with a high ridge standing upon it and a lake each side of it. All of this is moving steadily across the sea. We cannot understand it. Can you tell us what it is?'

'I am no lady now,' I replied, 'as you can see. So why do you ask me?'

There was an uncomfortable silence. When I spoke again it was with quiet authority.

'Nevertheless I can tell you what you saw. The men from my land, the Island of the Mighty, have heard of my terrible treatment and are coming to avenge me.'

I could feel a dread come on the assembly.

'But what is the forest that floats above the waves?' asked the messenger, his voice faltering.

'The bristling masts and yardarms of their ships.' I replied.

'And what is the mountain that moves beside the ships?'

I laughed shortly.

'What do you think?' I asked. 'It is Bran, my brother, wading across the sea.'

Again the men quailed.

'What is the high ridge on the mountain?'

'Bran's nose.'

'And what are the lakes to left and right of it?'

'His two eyes bent in anger on this land.'

There was now white fear on the men's faces. I glanced down at my apron and rubbed shreds of fatted flour between my fingers.

'He comes in great fury,' I said.

After they dismissed me I stayed in the main body of the palace and witnessed the panic, the hurried orders, the desperate comings and goings of messengers. Matholwch sent urgent word throughout the land and called up all the fighting men of Erin. They gathered quickly and held hasty council for already news had come that Bran and his force had reached the eastern shore. They decided to retreat behind the River Shannon and destroy the bridge that crossed it.

I heard these orders being shouted, and I knew why they were making this decision. Beneath the river's waters there were loadstones that grounded any ship that tried to sail across it. Without its bridge the Shannon was impassable.

As soon as the decision was made, hundreds of men swarmed down to the bridge and began dismantling it with ropes and pulleys. It was a job that should have taken several weeks, but somehow the men managed to pull it down in a few days. When they had finished, half the wooden struts that had held the bridge were piled up and sticking through the water, nevertheless the Shannon was now impossible to cross.

Matholwch was pleased, and thought for a while he had outwitted Bran, or at least stalled his onslaught. Then I heard a terrified servant shouting:

'Bran has become a bridge! Bran has become a bridge!'

Reports were coming in thick and fast that Bran was stretched full-length across the River Shannon. He was covered with hurdles and the army was advancing across his body.

As soon as he heard this news Matholwch worked fast. When the army had passed over and Bran was on his feet again, a company of messengers from the palace came thundering on horseback towards him.

'My lord,' they called out. 'The High King wishes nothing but good fortune to you!'

They brought their horses to a standstill beside him and looked up into his face. His eyes were like darting spears, his skin flushed red with effort and fury.
The men tried again:

'To recompense you for the wrong he has done your sister, the High King offers to invest your sister's son, your nephew, with the kingship of the land.'

Bran still stood towering above them, moving no muscle nor giving any sign that he had heard them.

'Matholwch also promises to stand down as king, and asks only that some provision is made for him either here or in the Island of the Mighty,' they said.

Bran shifted.

'As I have not been offered the kingship for myself,' he said curtly, 'I shall have to call my council and consider your proposals. And perhaps by that time I might receive a better offer.' He added drily: 'In fact we shall not give you an answer until you can offer better terms.'

The messengers promised to return with the best terms they could get and asked Bran to wait. Bran said he would only wait a short time, so they would need to return quickly.

As soon as his answer reached the court I was taken to the robing room and dressed again in my former gowns and finery. All the old courtesies were shown to me and I was invited to join the council. As I entered the hall the men were already in hot debate.

'Should we make peace with Bran?' they were asking each other, 'or should we join battle with him?'

As I listened, it soon became clear that half of the council were for fighting and half for making peace.

While the voices were raised in hot debate, I thought again of the two lands and of Bran's great dream of joining them in harmony. I thought of my old land – the deer-rich forests, the tumbled valleys, the spiked mountains and the heather-spread moors. Then I thought of my new land, the tangle of briar and woodland, the little rutted roads that ran between the sheep-filled meadows, the cracks and spills of streams across the mountains. I heard a man ask:

'How ready are our forces?'

There was an urgent murmuring of voices.

As they debated, a pall fell across the pictures in my head. I saw smoke rising from woodland clearings, huts springing into flame, stone hearths burned out and screaming children fleeing through the trees. I saw rivers blocked with bodies of men and jagged piles of bloodstained armour.

'Are there any terms he would accept?'

I returned abruptly from my vision. The voice was Matholwch's.

Murmuring followed, then I heard a man say:

'There is only one choice. We must show him honour by building him a house.'

'But the scale of it would be enormous!' a voice protested.

'Yes, indeed. It would have to be big enough to hold both him and his army in one half, and our men in the other. But it must be done,' said the first man, 'and after that we must offer him the kingship.'

In the silence that followed, I pushed my hands together, balancing the fingers tip to tip. It was a small movement, but enough to turn the men's eyes towards me.

'That would indeed honour my brother. It would be the first time he has ever fitted into a house,' I said quietly.

Matholwch stared at me, surprised. I could almost hear what he was thinking, and it showed how little he understood me. He thought I would want my brother to avenge me and lay the land waste.

After that I thought that the decision had been made. But then more messengers burst in with the news that the gathering warriors of Erin were eager to join battle. And so the debate turned again. Once more, in my mind's eye, I saw the two lands gashed with crimson streams and rivers, the plains scarred with mountainous heaps of pallid corpses.

As the images flared across my vision, pain reared in my breast. I tried to speak but my voice was drowned in a well of anguish.

'Oh, build the house!' I cried out at last. 'For the sake of my son and all the kingdom, build the house and keep the lands at peace!'

I went on arguing. I begged the council not to join war with Bran. It took all my strength, all my humility, my desperate pleading, to make them listen. But at last they agreed. Messengers were sent to Bran with the offer of a house and kingship and, after holding council with his men, he accepted the terms.

VII

I WATCHED the house as it was being built. I saw how huge it was, how sturdy. High pillars rose to the towering dome of the roof, a hundred wooden posts upholding the airy structure like rows of living trees.

When it was finally finished, a day was set for Gwern's Investiture as king. The morning of the ceremony was a bright one and Bran and his men set out in their finest clothes and began marching towards the house. They were making a stately pace as befitted the occasion, but my half-brother Efnisien hurried ahead, making sure he was the first to enter the house. He went in and looked about suspiciously, examining everything with a ruthless glare. Immediately he noticed something strange. There was a huge peg fixed to every pillar of the house and hanging from it, swinging slightly, was a heavily loaded leather bag.

'What is in this bag?' he asked one of the men of Erin.

'Only flour, my friend,' answered the man.

Efnisien reached up and moved his hand along the outside of the bag. He could feel the figure of a man lying within it. Efnisien ran his fingers along the bag until he found the man's head. He took hold of it through the leather and squeezed it until he crushed the brain. Then he went from pillar to pillar asking what each bag contained and crushing each head as he went. In this way he quietly squeezed to death two hundred hidden men.

When Bran and his company arrived, they were in good spirits. As they thronged into the hall at one end, the company of Erin entered at the other. A fire was lit in the centre of the house and wax candles were burning on the walls. A band of musicians struck up and played vigorously until the men had found their places. As soon as they were all seated I came in carrying Gwern in my arms. I set the young boy down in the middle of the host and for a brief moment there was peace between the two companies. With solemn ceremony the kingship was conferred upon Gwern and then Bran signalled for the boy to come to him. Gwern ran over and received an embrace. Then Manawydan called for him. The boy ran to him willingly and he, too, embraced him. Then Efnisien called him.

No one was prepared for what happened next. As soon as the boy reached Efnisien, he lifted him by his feet and dashed him headfirst into the fire. There was a moment of shock, a moment when time seemed stuck. But in that moment the fire began to devour my son. I was the first to react. In blind grief I hurled myself after him, but Bran was too quick for me. He caught me, lifted me in the air and held me locked between his shield and his breast. I beat my fists against him, flailing my arms and legs, bruising my body against the man-sized sheath of iron. Through my crazed grief I heard him shouting:

'Dogs of Gwern, beware Pierced Thighs!'

Then I heard men running for their armour, and after that the overwhelming din, the sound of clanging weapons rising in the enclosure of the house. Blazing with anguish, I emptied myself in screams until my whole body was drained.

All around me I could hear the terrible noise, the clash and groan of battle. I knew it well. The screams that greeted sudden woundings, the dreadful moans of warriors gored beyond mending. When Bran at last dropped me to the ground, I made my way between the trampling feet, the whirling sword blades. I crawled out of the house and into the wet hollow of a ditch. But even as I sank down, the warriors broke out of the house and raged towards me. As I had seen in my visions, they began savaging the land. Gripped by frenzied fighting, they fell upon whole villages, firing the huts, the trees, the standing crops, and slaughtering the people as they went.

When night came at last and pulled a veil over the dreadful land, hundreds of dead warriors lay strewn across the plains. Bran's troops were winning but we parleyed with the men of Erin and agreed a temporary truce until the sunrise.

Then, while our men were resting and recovering from the battle, a strange vision appeared on the horizon. A small but intense fire was glowing vivid red and, hanging above it, was a huge black-bellied object. Men were lifting bodies from a nearby mound of corpses, heaving them up and throwing them into the dark bowl. I knew at once what it was. So did Bran. His face went taut with horror. We watched them work all night. Then, as the thin light of dawn approached, we began to see them, ghost men climbing from the cauldron, animated corpses moving their stiffened arms and legs, limbering up for battle.

As the sun drew light across the sky, Bran gathered the men again into their ranks. They stood impatient, waiting for the onslaught. It was then the dead men started coming towards us, marching in silence, moving their jaws as if in battle-roar. But no sound came from them. The dumb ones moved swiftly, their purpose nothing but war and fighting. As they drew nearer, we saw the dull stare of their lightless eyes.

When our men joined battle with them there were no screams, no dying groans, no cries of bravery or triumph from this spectral army. Instead they hacked their noiseless way through our ranks, with no sound but the working of their armour. Even so, our side slaughtered more that day than before.

Next morning at the first faint light the dreaded ghost army came again. This time they were more of them. Our men fought determinedly but such warriors were harder to overcome than living men. Also, as we despatched more and more of the living army, we knew next day there would be more ghostly warriors coming after us.

Crouched among the battle slaughter, I slowly began to understand what had happened. The treasure of the land, the cauldron, had become corrupt. Now it was only a vessel of revival. No food issued from its mouth, and no new life. All it could do was spit out pale-faced, soulless warriors stripped of the word – the force of spirit.

Bran was heartstruck with grief, realising at last how he'd betrayed the land by giving up the cauldron. Beside him, Efnisien, too, began to see his terrible revenges for what they were – the darkness of a warrior's soul. As the deaths of his countrymen mounted with the cauldron's power, he felt a growing horror. Seized by anger and pain, he worked his way across the battlefield until he was among the men of Erin. Weaving through the wild dance of their weapons, he dropped down among their dead and lay there, waiting.

As soon as night descended Efnisien was thrown with the corpses into the cauldron. With the weight of the dead men pressed upon him, Efnisien stretched out his arms and legs and thrust them against its hot iron shell. He pushed out with all his strength, heaving against the walls while the pain mounted in his heart. He pushed until the vessels burst in his face and limbs. He pushed with all his might, heaving against the blistering walls. He gave a last great surge of effort and the cauldron burst apart, cracking into four huge pieces, which fell and twisted in the fire's heat. Efnisien's body fell with the other corpses into the furnace, his heart already stretched to breaking.

VIII

AFTER THE destruction of the cauldron, the victory was ours. But it was a bitter victory. Out of all our great army only seven men remained. My brother Manawydan was one of them, as was Pryderi, Rhiannon's son, also Taliesin the poet. Bran himself was lying full length and shivering, the end of a poisoned spear still quivering in his ankle. His strength failing, he ordered the seven men to come to him.

'I am dying,' he said. 'But before I die you must cut off my head.'

This was greeted with loud protests, but Bran raised his hand.

'You must take my head with you and bury it in the White Hill in London with my face looking towards the land of Gaul. But you will linger long on the road to the White Hill. You will be seven years at Harlech and will feast with the head.'

Though faint, his voice rose as if in ecstasy.

'And the head will entertain you. The Birds of Rhiannon will be singing for you in that place! From Harlech you will go to Gwales in Penvro, to a royal hall where you will again feast and be entertained by the head.'

He was almost crying now, trying to catch at his life before it left him.

'And you will stay there for eighty long years. You will feast and be happy and the head will not decay nor will the years weigh upon you until the door that must not be opened is opened by one of you. After that you must move swiftly to the White Hill, and bury the head.'

When he had delivered his message, Bran sank down looking mutely at me. I stretched myself across his breast and wept. With a great effort he lifted his arm and laid it over my back. I felt it tighten round me a moment and then fall loose.

As his great limbs began to stiffen, I was rolled away by one of the men. There was a swift flash of silver and then I saw the men were lifting up the head. Blood was pouring from the neck but the eyes were moving.

As instructed, we took Bran's head with us across the sea and came ashore at Ynis Mon. It was strange to be in my old country once again. My eyes took in the land that stretched away on either side. I stared around in disbelief while a terrible understanding came upon me. The pall of another slaughter lay across it. An unseen force had come against it, a terrible magic that had despatched the guardians of the land. The Island of the Mighty had become a wasteland.

Again I was seized again by my dreadful vision – the body of the land gashed with wounds, the plains scarred with corpse heaps, the life-blood of the land, the streams and rivers choked with warriors' bones and jagged armour, the wells and springs poisoned with blood, the forests burnt out and blackened, the children lifeless. Then I heard the women keening and crying. Crying against the waste, the battle madness. The women whose voices blew out on the wind and lost their forming. The women who prophesied aloud. The women whose mouths were stopped, whose wombs were used for warrior-making.

I felt my heart beating against its squeezing, beating like a drum against the hollow womb, the empty cauldron. Efnisien's heart broke splitting the burning iron. And now my heart was breaking with the vision of the shattered cauldron. As I sank down into the darkness I thought I could hear my own voice faintly, oh so faintly:

> I shall sing upon a starling
> Sing my song
> About a cauldron that was lost and broken
> Sing my song.

The plaintive verse sang out across the desolation, endlessly echoing and repeating. It seemed as if it would never leave the place, as if the land would never be whole again. But then I heard another song cut across the first, bringing another rhythm, like a lone horse gathering speed across the plain.

The cauldron is broken
and I lie dead.
The magic sings
in my brother's head.

The new refrain took hold and thrummed the earth, waking the sleeping seeds, the tiny life forms.

I understood then what it was. I knew then, as I sank into the coldness of the earth, that the time of men had come. I knew that Bran would hold the magic, guarding it until my power returned, until the Mother rose again to heal the land.

For the head of Bran the Blessed was the cauldron now.

Brighid the Mother

*My festival is Imbolc 'in womb' time, so besides being the Maiden, I am
also the Mother who bears the burden of the coming spring.*

THIS IS my lineage. I am the daughter of the Dagda, the Good God,
king of the Tuatha de Danaan, the faerie people. With them I came,
blown in a magic mist across the sea to Erin. But the mist was the far-
furled smoke of our ships as we burned them on the western shores of
Connemara. For we pledged ourselves to that land and swore we would
never turn our faces towards the sea again. And so we shared that land
with the Fomorians, the ancient giant race who lived there.

When I had grown to womanhood, my father married me to
King Bres. Bres the Beautiful he was called. And, though half-
Fomorian, he was fair indeed – no giant but a flower of a man. It should
have been a good match, one that would foster peace between our two
races. And I, the shining child, was to be the peacemaker.

And so I went, the luminous bride in my crystal white gown
with snowdrops in my yellow hair, and lay with the man of perfect form
in the bridal bed. But though it was with the goddess of fertility that he
lay – with the shining one, the fiery woman of passion and desire and
beauty, yet he saw only my whiteness, my virginity. He took me as a
possession and used me harshly.

For Bres was flawed. His heart was hard as flint and he was
cruel not only to me, but to my people.

First he laid heavy taxes on them, levying dues on every hearth,
every kneading-trough, and every quern. Then he laid a poll-tax of an
ounce of gold on every person. As if this was not enough, he cheated my

people, asking only for the milk of the brown and hairless cows and, when this was agreed, singeing all the cattle between the two fires at Beltain and then claiming all their milk as his due. As to his treatment of the cattle, I felt the pain of it in the two breasts of my body, for, in former times, the cattle were under my care – the care of the Mother Goddess, and their milk was a gift from my hand.

Then Bres set my father, the Dagda, to work, making him labour as a common man, building raths and digging trenches. And then my brother the god Ogma, he of the silver tongue, father of the mystic art of poetry, was forced to carry bundles of firewood.

And this was the first spearing of my heart. For it is I who breathe life into the word, who foster inspiration and creativity in all the arts.

But worse was to come. For, while I lived in the palace, with my light shrouded, my joy wasted, my gifts unused, Bres laid a pall upon my people. On his orders, no bard who came to the king's court was given courtesy or hospitality. No grease sat upon his knife, and no ale upon his breath. Neither the poets, the bards, the harpers, pipers, jugglers, athletes, nor the fools were welcomed. And when Cairbre the chief poet of my people, who was used to being treated with great honour, came to visit Bres, he was housed in a low, dark cabin with no fire to warm himself and not even a bed to lie on. Just three small dry cakes were brought to him on a tiny dish. So outraged was Cairbre by this treatment that, at first light, he went out and pronounced this satire against the king:

> Without food served upon a dish,
> Without the milk of a cow which feeds a calf
> Without hospitality for a man in the dark night
> Without pay for a company of bards
> Let that be the plight of Bres
> Let there be no increase for him.

Cairbre's poem was the first satire ever made in Ireland. And the power of his satire, the poetic power that Bres scorned, took hold of the king and raised boils upon his face. Thus he became so marred and disfigured that he was forced to abdicate the kingship, being no longer perfect in his form.

Then Bres left the palace in disgrace and disfigurement. But even after he went, the Formorians still levied their harsh taxes on my people. Meanwhile Bres went to seek out his long lost father, hoping with his help to muster an army from among his Fomorian kin. And so at last, aided by his mother, he found out where his father lived in the land of the Fomorians and went to him.

'What has brought you to me from the land over which you ruled?' asked his father.

'Nothing, replied Bres, 'but my own pride and lack of justice. I have levied taxes and taken the prize possessions of a people who have never been under such constraints before.'

'What you have done is bad indeed,' said his father. 'It would have been better for you to rule a prosperous people and to receive prayers instead of curses. But you already know this, so why have you come to me?'

'Father, I have come to ask you for champions,' said Bres, 'for I plan to take back my throne by force.'

'You should not regain by injustice what you did not first gain by justice,' replied his father.

'Then what advice would you give me?' countered Bres, undaunted.

And so determined was he and so persistent that, though his father was sorrowful and angry at his behaviour, he finally gave in, and sent him first to Balor of the Baleful eye who lived on Tory Island, and afterwards to Indech, the king of the Fomorians, and both offered him their support.

Over the next few years, Bres raised a great army and prepared to march on the Tuatha – the people of his former kingdom. And, as the bards and poets now relate, never before had an army descended upon Ireland more terrible than the host that Bres raised against us.

And that was the second spearing of my heart. For I, Brighid, saw and suffered all this under his hand. I, who champion a people of the arts, a people of music, of storytelling, of fire, of feasting and fast-flowing ale.

But yet there was hope for us. Bright hope came to us even as Bres began mustering his troops. For a new god came to the Tuatha – Lugh the young sun lord, brilliant to behold, with burning hands and flame-dripping golden hair, wielding a spear of fire. He appeared at the Assembly of our gods and rulers and dazzled us with his skills. So, straightaway, Nuada of the Silver Hand, who had taken the kingship after Bres, stepped down and gave him the throne.

Then, under Lugh's leadership we planned our warfare, for seven long years we planned it and made our weapons. And, at Lugh's command, the three powers that are mine – the arts of smithcraft, healing and poetry, became the chief arts that we used against the Fomorians.

This is how we planned to use them:

First Goibniu, the smith, promised to forge magical weapons for my people – swords spears and javelins:

'No spear-point which shall be forged by my hand shall miss its target,' he declared, 'and no flesh it pierces shall survive.'

He made this pledge in the heat of his furnace and in the power of his craft and his making.

Then Diancecht, the physician, pledged himself to heal my people:

'Every man who is wounded I will make whole on the following day,' he said. 'Every man, that is, who has not lost his head, or broken his spine.'

And afterwards Cairbre, the poet, pledged himself to use the *glam dicenn,* the magic power of satire:

'I will wield it like a biting sword upon the enemy,' he said, 'and raise such shame among them that they offer no resistance.'

And I, Brighid, bearing the mantle of Danu the Great Mother of the Tuatha, breathed these three powers, my three arts, into my people so that they would win the great battle.

And after battle was joined, Goibniu the smith kept fashioning new weapons in the heat of my fire, and, in that same heat, Luchta the wright made the spearshafts, and Credne the brazier added the rivets in three quick turns and cast the spear rings on them so that they held fast. And because of this, there were always weapons and spears in plentiful supply, and each possessed a keen magic.

Also, as the battle raged, those of our people that were slain were carried to my healing well, the Well of Slane – whose waters were sweetened with every herb that grows in Erin, and cast into it. And while they were there the two sons of Diancecht together with his daughter Airmed sang spells over them. And the power of the invocation of the spells hovering over the healing waters restored our dead warriors to life.

Meanwhile the spears and swords of the enemy became broken and blunted and there were none to replace them. And when their men died they were not seen on the field again. So when the Fomorians saw that our weapons were unblunted and our dead were rising up again, they appointed a spy to find the cause of it. And the man they chose was my son Ruadan.

Ah, Ruadan, my child! My only legacy from a cold king! Ruadan, the babe who once gave his mother joy in a palace empty of song and laughter. Ruadan, who saw the parting of ways between his mother and his father, who looked from one to the other, who reached the threshold of his manhood, the time of his dreadful choosing – and caused the last and greatest spearing of my heart!

Ruadan came to the place where the weapons were being forged, and saw the work of Goibniu and the others. He heard the incantations and saw the healing Well of Slane. Then he stole away to the camp of the Fomorians and reported all these things to his father. And Bres sent him onto the battlefield again with a secret and terrible mission, to kill Goibniu, my magic smith.

Then Ruadan came into the smithy with an innocent look on his young face and asked for a spear. And, because he was my son and three-parts Tuathan, my people gave him one gladly. Then Ruadan took it and weighed it in his hands as if to test its strenth, then suddenly turned and hurled the spear at Goibniu, wounding him in the chest. But Goibniu took hold of the weapon and pulled it out of himself and, with the warm blood flowing from his wound, hurled it back with such force that it pierced right through Ruadan. Then Goibniu plunged into the well and healed himself.

But in the last of his strength, Ruadan dragged himself to the Fomorian camp. There he fell at the feet of Bres, his father, with the spear struck through his body like a bolt. And there he died.

When I heard that my son had died, I ran to the smithy and implored Goibniu to lay him in the well of healing. But Goibniu refused. He said my son had sided with the enemy and exposed our secret, so he deserved to die. I wept in all the desperate agony of a mother, and begged Goibniu to save his life, but all my tears and entreaties came to nothing. At last, in my grief and despair I wandered onto the battlefield.

Then, on the battlefield, my keening, the caoine *of Brighid for her son, was the first lament to be heard in the whole of Erin. The mother shrieking and keening for her child. The mother keening for her child. The mother first shrieking, then wailing, then weeping for her child, the child too soon returned to earth.*

My shrieking and my keening were for the loss of my son – the deepest and cruellest spearing of my heart. Yet my weeping was also for his betrayal of my people – the people of our Mother Danu. For Ruadan had forsaken the way of the Mother and pledged himself to his father.

This I could not understand. For it was the rule of his father Bres that stopped the mouths of the bards and poets throughout the land, that silenced the horns and pipes, that dumbed the harpstrings and let the fire die within the feasting hall. And it was Bres who sent Ruadan to kill Goibniu, wielder of magic, guardian of my sacred fire, forger of my sunbright spears. And it was Bres who, on the word of my son, ordered his men to carry stones to the Well of Slane and block the healing waters of my well, so that the dead could no longer be revived.

It was after the death of my son and the stopping up of my well, that Lugh took charge. He escaped from the nine men sent to guard him and thundered down onto the battlefield in his chariot. There he began heartening our army, inspiring them to greater deeds of prowess, urging them to victory and the breaking of their bondage. Led by Lugh, our army came charging against the Fomorians with a great shout. Glory and slaughter were the order of the day. Red blood spouting over white skin, bravery and losses, greatness of courage, high and valorous deeds and everywhere the dreadful clamour of war.

At the battle's height Lugh came face to face with the giant Balor – he of the single baleful eye, the eye that needed four men to lift the hooded lid, the eye that could destroy whole armies with one glance. Lugh, his grandson, met him in the middle of the field.

'Lift up my eyelid!' called the fearful giant to his men, 'lift it up so I can see this Babbler – this so-called king of the Tuatha!'

The whole army looked away as the lid was lifted. But as soon as the terrible eye was open, Lugh raised his sling and aimed a sharp stone at it. He threw it with such force that it drove the eye right into the giant's head and out through the back of it so that its power fell upon the Fomorian forces.

After Lugh had overcome the dark and ancient power of the giant – a deed that was long ago foretold, and after he had brought his force of light onto the field, the battle became a rout. Now we could hear the Morrigan with her two sisters screaming above the armies, raising battle frenzy, rousing our troops and harrying and confusing the enemy. Then we saw Ogma and Indech fighting to the death in dreadful single combat and falling together, we saw Bres captured, pleading for his life and being spared by Lugh. All this we saw, until finally, in a rush of strength and fury, our people pushed the Fomorians back, driving them down towards the sea from whence they came, and forcing their surrender.

Such was our victory, but the cost was great. For, in the wake of battle, the heaped corpses that lay pale as snow on the ground were as numerous as the spill of stars in a black sky.

Early next morning, in the spear light of the new day, I went out and walked on the blood-soaked battlefield among the ruins of my people. And my heart bled as I looked on the twisted faces of the dead, for I knew that the end-time of the Mother had begun.

Yet I am the goddess who endures. Maiden of the spring am I, and also Mother. Protecter of women in the pangs of childbirth, and midwife to the sacred son, the Mabon. And it was Lugh and not my son who carried my torch and led the people of the Goddess Danu against the oppression of the Fomorians. For my Mother time was done.

But I, Brighid, am also Seer and Wise Woman. And so I went, in my Crone form, into the darkness.

MACHA

I did not speak to him until after we had slept together. I had been watching him for some time. I thought he was beautiful, neither young nor old. He was a widower living alone except for four sons, each now beginning to go their own way. He was wealthy, too, a cow-lord. My name means 'pastureland'. My green mantle is rough-threaded as the stubbled grasses of the mountainside. I wished the cow-lord to graze upon me.

CRUNNCHU WAS sitting on the couch looking out at the white peaks of the mountains when I came to him. I entered his house in silence. Without a sound I slipped in through the doorway.

I knew, even before I came, that I would be all his longing – for I was all that he looked on from the window of his house. My face was white, my eyes blue as the lakes in the mountains, my hair like the dark combing of pines climbing the pale slopes.

He stirred when he saw me but did not rise, perhaps because of the stillness that was in me. Without a word I sat beside him. My green cloak was wrapped around my pale young body; it rose and fell with my breathing. On and on we sat. No noise, no move was made between us. As the sun went down his eyes became faint stars, glittering in the gloom. I got up then. I knelt to the fire and parted the ashes to lift the flames. I watched as the flames reared up unbridled.

Then I went into the kitchen and sifted the flour with a handful of fat. I worked the dough on the kneading trough and left it to rise. In the last of the light I took a pitcher and went into the field. I pulled the teats of the cow and brought back milk. Still at that time no word had passed between us.

When I re-entered the house I turned about once, sunwise.

Then I instructed the servants to prepare the meal. We ate in the dumb light of the candles, Crunnchu's grey eyes fixed upon me. His face was like a mountain crag. His limbs were spare and strong beneath his garments.

When our meal was finished the servants departed to their beds. I went again to the fire and banked it with ashes to tame it until the morning. Then I turned in a sunwise circle again and went upstairs. I found him lying on his bed. Slowly I lay down beside him. I touched his skin. Wordlessly, soundlessly I stroked the man until I felt his body quiver under my pale fingers.

·····

I STAYED with Crunnchu. Though he was no king, his body was a delight to me. And if he had prospered before I came to him, now he prospered even more. I brought increase to his pastureland, his cattle yield, his crops. But our love was secret. It was not for men to know that Crunnchu was living with a woman of the *sidhe*.

And so our life was solitary. Alongside the servants, we worked the land together. We milked the cattle and we minded the sheep drifting up the mountainside. In spring we tilled the fields, in summer we harvested the crops. In autumn we pressed ourselves against the flanks of the horses and drummed the earth, racing across the fallow pastures at the mountain's roots. And, soon enough my body, too, swelled with the fruits of our fertility.

Then came the day of the Great Assembly. Like all the other farmers in the district, Crunnchu was planning to travel to Ulster to attend it. I felt a prick of fear. I caressed him as if for the last time. I took his two hands and kissed them, I let the tears run from my eyes on his breast. I warned him of the dangers. I reminded him that if he spoke my secret, it would be the end of our union.

'Don't worry, I will say nothing,' he promised, taking my face between his hands, and kissing away my tears. Then he mounted his horse and was gone, eager for the games and races, the tournaments, the costumes, the processions.

After he had gone, I sat beside the fire and felt the heartbeats in my swollen belly.

Several days later I was woken by loud shouts and banging on the door. I pulled my cloak round my shoulders and went slowly down to open it.

Two men stood there looking as if they had flung themselves through the wind to reach me. As soon as he mastered his breath one cried out:

'Lady, we have been sent to fetch you.'

'Why?' I asked.

'The king has imprisoned your husband and will not release him until you come.'

The other messenger broke in:

'The king desires you to race his horses.'

'Yes,' said the first man. 'It is because your husband boasted that you could outrun them.'

'My husband has spoken rashly,' I said.

In a flash I saw Crunnchu, his eyes bright with drink. I saw him scorning the king even as he made the crowd raise their glasses to his champion horses. I saw Crunnchu yielding to the forceful rearing of the liquor, bragging to his fellows, spilling my secret. I heard the forbidden words burst from him and gallop round the table, rising in volume as each man took up the taunt, repeating in drunken incredulity:

'My wife can run faster than those horses! My wife can run faster than those horses!'

Then I saw the look on the king's face.

But now the men were trying to hurry me. One took hold of my arm. I broke away.

'My husband has spoken rashly,' I said again.

'Nevertheless you must come,' said the messengers.

A whip-flick of fear touched my belly.

'But I am not fit to run,' I protested. 'Look at me. I am about to give birth!'

'If you refuse to come,' they said, 'the king will kill your husband.'

I saw I had no choice. And so I went with the men to the Great Assembly.

·····

WHEN I arrived the crowds were waiting impatiently for me. Word had gone round that there was to be a new race ordered by the king, and they could not understand the delay. I sensed they were in unruly mood after so many days of drinking. As we made our way through the crowd I saw Crunnchu at the far end of the field. He was standing gagged between two soldiers, his wrists and ankles bound with ropes.

I went onto the plain. My cloak was tossed aside and my dress fell over my belly. My belly was full and rounded for all to see. Two babes lay curled within it.

I strode up to the king and addressed him:

'Why have I been brought here?'

The crowd answered with a roar:

'You are to run against the two horses of the king!'

They were charged, like children, with the thrill of a novelty.

''But, look at me,' I cried, spreading out my hands, 'I am about to give birth!'

The crowd was silent for a moment. I could hear murmurings. I was counting on the compassion of the women. Then I heard the king's voice, booming, imperious. He was addressing the two soldiers who were holding Crunnchu.

'Unsheath your swords,' he commanded, 'and hew the man to death.'

I met Crunnchu's eyes. My heart exploded in a star of fear. I ran up and down the field of faces.

'Help me!' I cried.

I reached my arms towards them.

'Help me,' I cried again, 'My time is nearly on me.'

The men shuffled. Some of the women dipped their heads. Nevertheless, my hope rising, I pleaded with them again.

'Speak for me,' I begged.

The men's eyes were hard. The women kept their heads down and refused to look at me. I could not believe their cruelty.

'Protect me!' I cried. 'Spare me for the love of your mothers.'

The crowd stood silent, uneasy. They were hearing me but eyeing the king. Not a murmur came from them now.

Tears were streaming down my face. I reached my hands out to them, my voice breaking in desperation.

'Think of your mothers!' I begged. 'Remember that each of you was born from a woman.'

I turned again to the king. Surely his heart would soften and then the crowd would turn.

'Oh King,' I pleaded, 'give me just a short delay. Let me first be delivered of my babes.'

My voice rang clear, then broke, swallowing itself. I was almost overcome with sobbing.

Before I could plead again he raised his hand. He spoke quietly into the silence.

'It shall not be so,' he said.

I looked round one last time at the crowd. The faces of the men were hard, the women's fearful, mixed with shame. Still they kept silent.

I knew now there was no help for me. The race had to be won against the king for love of the land, for love of Crunnchu. I looked at him, his eyes bright with grief, and the flame mounted in my heart, the fierce, determined fire of woman's willing.

I faced the king boldly. My voice rang out for all to hear:

'Shame on you!' I cried.

'Shame on you for showing no respect! Shame on you for showing no pity! Because of this, a heavy burden will fall upon the land of Ulster.'

A flicker of fear ran across the king's face. He called out:

'What is your name?'

I spoke my name then. I called it out aloud, together with my secret lineage.

'Macha,' I said, 'the daughter of Sainreth mac Imbaith, 'The Strange One of the Ocean.'

The king paused at this. I thought again he might relent. But his face remained impassive.

Now it was I who gave the orders.

I called out: 'Bring on the horses!'

Then the king's prize stallions were brought onto the field and yoked to his fastest chariot. I heard their blowing and the brittle tinkling as they pulled against their bits and bridles. I felt their excitement mounting. They were dancing on the field, impatient to run against me. I threw off my cloak and went to crouch beside them.

The signal was given. Whips touched their flanks and the horses sprang forward. I spurted forward with them. My hair blew back against my neck, my legs were leaping, keeping pace with the thumping hooves, the rattling chariot. My belly ran before me, the unborn babes crunching together. My heart was drumming a deafening rhythm, banging its urgency across the land. The riders chafed their steeds, lashing them onwards; only the will of woman chafed me, and the wild horse spirit. I pressed my long neck forward, keeping level with the streaming stallions.

We rounded the field once.

In the middle of the second round my pains came on me, rearing across my belly like sudden thunder, mounting in banded waves like tightening straps, then breaking across my womb in strikes of lightning. Still I ran. Still I kept head to head with the thrusting stallions. By the third lap they were straining forward, spindles of spittle flowing from their iron-ringed mouths. The lightning was cracking through my body, opening fissures in my belly. The babes were knocking at each other, bone to bone. Yet still I ran, my woman's heart stretched now to bursting. Womb-leaked blood and water was streaming down my legs yet still I ran. My feet were slipping on the turf, my wet hair painted to my neck. The horses' heads flashed up and down beside me, whipped by the driver, spurting forward for the finish. Out flew my legs, my feet now whirling with the dancing of the land, its fertile song, its forceful thrumming. I saw the line stretched before me. I had almost reached it when I slipped and skidded. Carried by the wetted grass, I slid across it, one hand's breadth before the king's sweat-streaming horses.

No sound of cheering greeted me as I lay heaving on the ground, nothing but the hammer of blood within my ears. The only sign of my triumph was Crunnchu's release. He ran towards me and knelt down mouthing lamentations that I could not hear. Meanwhile the unpitying crowd was beginning to disperse, the men were fussing with their cloaks, the women gathering up their belongings.

All at once I heard a mighty scream. It travelled round the field and split the ears of all the people. I thought it came from somewhere far away. I did not realize it was spilling from my mouth.

With the terrible screaming I could feel my babes being born. The blood was rearing in my ears and rushing across my brain. Before the light left me, I shouted desperate words into the silence. If I could not reach the women, I had to make the men's hearts listen. I had to turn them into women.

'Because of this outrage,' I shouted, 'I lay on all you men the dreadful pains of woman! For five days all you warriors of Ulster must bear the pangs of woman's labour!'

The blackness was hovering over me. There were only broken threads of light remaining.

'And may they come upon you, ' I cried. 'May they come on you when you would ride to war, when you would ravage the land, when you would lay waste its people and its cattle!'

My voice was weaker. The light was now a spear-prick. With a **final thrust I called out:**

'When your urge is to go to war, may you be prevented by the pangs of birthing!'

For a moment my words danced like a string of jewels in the stillness. Then darkness tumbled like the night upon me.

But all the warriors of Ulster heard me. And from that time, nine generations of them bore the pangs of women. When the land was attacked, and their will was to go to battle, all the Flower of Ulster lay on their beds and suffered woman's groaning.

And after that time, the place of the Great Assembly, the plain of the dreadful Shaming of the Mother, that place was called Emain Macha. It was named for the girl child and the boy, the 'Twins of Macha' that were born there.

Rhiannon

Out of the night I come. Pale is my horse as the moon, my robe gold as the sun. I ride from one world into another, from dark into light, shaking death from my tail. Life streams from my hard hoof, my muscled body, my spindled legs, my bellowing breath, my high-arched cry.

I am Rig Antona, Queen Most High,
I am white mare of the land.
I have come to woo a king.

The king I want has ruled the World Above and guarded the World Below. His name is Pwyll. But my father would bridle me, would tether me to another consort. Nevertheless my feet are bare under my gold robe. Clinging to my mare's flanks, they merge with her swiftness. Beneath my royal robes I am my own woman . . . .

'A FINE lady on a white horse'. That is how I appeared to the Lord of Dyfed, when he sat himself on the Mound of Arberth. Pwyll had dared to climb that magic hill, knowing that when he sat upon it one of two things would come upon him – either a blow or a marvel. And so he sat down with great ceremony surrounded by his courtiers, and waited.

What was it to be? Something wonderful and magical, or some nameless horror, testing and terrible? The daring of it made Pwyll feel vibrantly alive. A finger of wind passed along his neck, ran across his scalp. He sat in silence and waited. He waited until the sun went down in an orange splash behind the hill and the mound stood out like an upturned cauldron.

In a strip of peeled sunlight I appeared. A fine lady on a white horse, indeed. I had rings on my fingers, and from my three birds came a sweet music, pervasive as perfume. Far-off and near were my birds, hard to catch with mortal eyes, their singing like a pulse, a feather-beat. Chiming against its subtle melody, a brittle music came from the bell-like trappings of my mare fluttering in the twilight air.

I was Pwyll's marvel.

The king saw the luminous glow of my horse, the twin flames of her ears, and a forgotten image stirred in his mind. Like a man caught in a dream he sent one of his men to stop me. The man ran after me but I drew away. I was floating, my mare's legs gathered in a stately trot. The man went to fetch his horse. He whipped it to speed and pounded after me. But still my stately trot outpaced him. When both horse and rider grew tired and gave up the chase, I rounded the hill and was taken from sight.

The next evening Pwyll braved the magic mound again, as I knew he would. Again I appeared. This time his man had a horse ready. As soon as he saw me he sprang on its back and came after me. Still I floated forward in my dreamlike trotting – always just out of reach. The man began with a trot, then speeded up, exerted all his strength, whipping his horse to a frenzy before giving up in anger and disbelief. Then, again, I disappeared behind the hill.

The third night, as I expected, the king had his own horse ready. Round the hill I came, haloed like the moon, my gold robe blazing and my pale mare gently ambling. The king's horse was the swiftest in his stable. I heard the poor creature's panting breath behind me, I felt the ache of its full-stretched legs, the shuddering hooves. The king was urging it on, faster and faster. And yet I was always just ahead. I neither speeded up, nor stopped, nor turned my head until, at last, the king called:

'Lady, I beg you, for the love of the man that you hold most dear, stop for me!'

I floated to a halt, then turned and faced him.

'Gladly,' I said.

I looked at Pwyll. I looked at his horse. The king was pasted with sweat, his horse near to collapsing with exhaustion.

'And it would have been better for your horse had you called out earlier,' I added.

Pwyll was level with me now and so I withdrew my veil. I saw him start as I revealed my face. Sometimes the whiteness of my skin shines with its own glow. Sometimes my oak-brown eyes hold a fragile power. Sometimes my smooth mouth trembles at its corner. These things happen when I love a man.

After some moments Pwyll blurted out:

'Lady, where have you come from?'

Before I could answer he added:

'And where are you going?'

I smiled at his confusion.

'I have business of my own.' I said, 'several affairs that need my attention. But besides that,' I added, 'I am glad to see you.'

His confusion deepened. He was gazing at me as if I were a creature of a breed that he had never seen before. After a while he collected himself and said courteously:

'Lady, I welcome you!' His mouth widened in a smile.

And,' he added, 'I would like to know the nature of your business.'

'As to that,' I replied, my eyes never leaving his face, 'my most important task was to see you.'

'That is the best task you could possibly have,' he replied, his voice light with teasing flattery.

Feeling more confident of himself he moved his horse until it nudged my own, then he leaned towards me.

'What is your name?' he asked.

'I am Rhiannon, daughter of Heveydd the Old.' My voice rang like the sound of hooves striking on hollowed stone. I could hear its power, its music.

'I have come because I am being forced against my will to wed a man. If I have a choice, I choose you, but if you refuse me, I will consent to marry him.'

I looked down and said softly:

'It is to hear your reply that I have come.'

I waited while he weighed my words.

When he spoke, his voice was hushed:

'By all the gods,' he said, 'if I had the choice of every woman in the world, I would choose you.'

My breath came back in a rush and, with it, a hurried order:

'Then, before I am given to this other man, you must arrange a time to meet with me again.'

'Make it whenever you like,' said Pwyll. 'The sooner it is, the more pleased I will be!' He was laughing like a boy.

'Then promise me you will come to the court of my father, Heveydd, a year from tonight. I will see to it that the wedding feast is ready.'

'You can be sure I will be there.' answered Pwyll, his eyes bright against the descending darkness.

'I must go now.' I said. 'Farewell, my lord! And don't forget your promise.'

Then I touched a foot to my horse, swung his head round, and rode away into the night.

Back into the Otherworld I ride. My moon-pale horse spreading its legs before me, my birds wheeling about my head, far and near. Birds that can raise a man from death, that can lull the living into death-like dreaming.

A man with hair dark as a blooded sun lifts his long arms and spreads his fingers. Black branches of bare trees wave with his hands. The land is empty.

The flanks of my mare quiver. We lie quiet, our hearts beating as one. We lie quiet for a year. And when the year is ended, we know our wedding feast is ready.

II

PWYLL, WHO had ridden boldly into the Otherworld once before, rode into my father's court on the day appointed with a retinue of ninety-nine men. A great feast had been prepared against his coming. The hall was decorated with branches of rowan and fragranced with scented lamps of honey-wax. Fresh green rushes were strewn about the floor, and scattered boughs of blossom. Messengers, servants, all the household of my father, ran about seeing to the business of the celebrations. The plates and goblets sat flaming on the long tables, lit by slips of sun from the long windows. The light peppered the grey spirals of my father's beard.

Heveydd the Old motioned to Pwyll to take the seat beside him. I wondered at my father's composure in the face of my defiance. I sat on the other side of Pwyll. I felt his eyes appraising me. My throat was swathed in jewelled golden strings. My breasts were held within the pointed halter-neck of my silver dress. From our twin crowns, like a multi-coloured robe, the guests flowed down the tables in order of rank. Savouries were carried in, samples for the tongue to toy with, presaging further dishes. The first tastings of wine came too, with pancakes of bread, and herb sauces for dipping.

After the first course there was a pause for conversation. Pwyll's eyes were twin goblets of wine spilling love and desire. I looked into them and saw in their gleaming curves the blood-haired man again, his long arms reaching out, his fingers feeling for me.

Then suddenly there he was striding down the hall, the red flames of his hair licking round his neck.

'The blessings of the gods attend you, my friend,' said Pwyll. 'Sit down with us!' he urged, waving a magnanimous hand.

'I will not,' replied the man, 'for I have come to ask a favour.'

'Then whatever it is, if it is in my power to grant it, I shall do so gladly,' said Pwyll, the warm wine trickling through his veins.

I caught Pwyll's arm, my heart thudding with anticipation.

'What have you said?' I cried. But my warning was too late. Already the young man's face was creased into a sneer.

'My Lady,' he said, turning his gleeful gaze upon me, 'all the court have heard his answer.'

Pwyll clung to his mood of good humour.

'What, Friend, is your request?' he asked.

The man gave a slow, measured smile.

'You will be sleeping tonight with the woman I love best in all the world,' he said. 'But it is her I have come for and, besides that, I request the feast and all the preparations.'

I saw a glance pass between the man and my father. Then I heard the intake of breath as Pwyll saw at a stroke all he had waited for, all his good fortune, all that he loved, drain away into a bottomless chasm.

'It is well that you say nothing!' I burst out angrily. 'I have never seen a more foolish display of wits!'

Pwyll's eyes were two black pits in his pale face.

'Lady, I did not know who he was!'

'This is Gwawl,' I said, 'a man of vast wealth and ruler of a great kingdom, the man my father would have me wed against my will.'

A wave of murmured concern flowed round the guests.

I turned again to Pwyll.

'As you have pledged your word,' I said quietly, 'you will have to give me to him, in order to maintain your honour.'

Pwyll was shaking.

'What kind of answer is that,' he said. 'I cannot make such an answer. I cannot bring myself to do it.'

Gwawl was already striding in triumph round the astonished guests. I bent towards Pwyll as if for a last embrace.

'Trust me,' I whispered. 'Give me to him as you have promised and I will make sure he never has me.'

'How will you do that?' asked Pwyll.

Then I told him my plan.

Gwawl finished strutting round the hall and confronted Pwyll again.

'Well, Lord,' he said, 'it is time you gave me an answer!'

Pwyll gave a deep sigh and gripped my wrist beneath the table.

'I shall grant whatever is in my power to give you,' he answered.

I rose at this.

'Friend, ' I said, 'concerning the feast and preparations, they have already been given to the soldiers and the people of our kingdoms, so they cannot be given to anyone else. But as for my own person, if you will return to this court a year from tonight, you shall have your own feast, and after that you may sleep with me.'

Then Gwawl returned to his kingdom and Pwyll passed through the gates of the worlds with his retinue of ninety-nine men, and a small sack that I had given him, and returned to Dyfed.

III

AFTER A year, the wedding feast was prepared again. But this time it was Gwawl who sat beside me. Gwawl with his lickings of red hair, and his thick red mouth lifting slightly at the corner. The first course was brought in and, with it, the first tastes of wine, as before. In the lull for conversation I watched the entrance at the end of the high hall. Presently a stooped figure came in. It was an old beggar wearing ragged garments and over-sized rag boots and carrying a bag in his hands. It took a long time for the man to shuffle the length of the hall but, at last, he came face to face with Gwawl. He bowed towards the ground and gave Gwawl a greeting.

'And the greetings of the gods to you, too' answered Gwawl.

'Lord,' said the old beggar, 'I have a request to make.'

Gwawl gave a short laugh.

'If it is reasonable,' he said, shooting me a glance, 'I will gladly grant it.'

'It is reasonable, lord, ' replied the other, 'for it is only to ward off a little hunger. My request is that you fill this small bag with food.'

'Why!' cried Gwawl, 'that is a modest request indeed and I will certainly grant it!'

Then he motioned to the attendants who came forward and began to fill the bag. But however much they stuffed it with food, the bag remained half empty.

'Friend,' cried Gwawl, 'will your bag never be full?'

'On my honour,' answered the beggar, 'it will not be full until a true ruler of land and possessor of riches treads the food down with his two feet and declares 'Enough has been put in here!'

I caught at Gwawl's sleeve.

'My lord, hurry and do what he says!' I urged. 'Quick, jump in the bag before the man removes the entire feast!'

'Gladly,' said Gwawl, jumping up. Soon he had his feet in the bag and was treading down the food with a vengeance, when with a swift, sly motion, the beggar pulled the bag over his head, turned it upside down, and closed the bag quickly, knotting its strings. Then the beggar straightened up, threw back his hood and put his horn to his lips.

At the blast, ninety-nine men came running from the orchard where they had been hiding, and charged into the high hall. They seized Gwawl's guests, marched them outside and put them under guard. Then Pwyll flung off his boots and ragged costume.

Meanwhile his men re-entered the hall. As each man came in, he struck the bag, kicking it or hitting it with his staff.

'What is in here?' he asked.

'A badger,' the other men replied.

'What game is being played?'

'Badger in the Bag!' they answered.

When the game had gone beyond endurance a voice cried out from inside the bag:

'Listen to me, lord! To die in a bag is not a noble thing!'

My father cut in:

'Listen to him. He speaks true enough.'

'I will take your advice,' said Pwyll, his eyes on mine.

I stood up.

'This is my advice,' I said, 'you are now the lord of this feast and it is for you to grant the requests of suppliants and entertainers. Request that Gwawl does this on your behalf. But, make him swear that he will make no claim against you nor seek revenge. If he agrees, that will be sufficient punishment for him.'

'I will do that gladly!' shouted the voice from the bag.

'And I, too, will accept such advice from Hevydd and Rhiannon,' answered Pwyll.

Then Gwawl was let out of the bag and his men were set free.

'Make sure he gives you some kind of security,' growled Hevydd, 'in fact, I can do it myself.'

Then Hevydd drew up a list of securities.

Afterwards Gwawl said to Pwyll:

'Now draw up your own terms!'

'I will abide by Rhiannon's terms,' Pwyll answered.

'Then let me go now, for I am bruised and wounded and need a healing bath,' said Gwawl.

And, with that, he left the court and returned to his own kingdom.

Once he was gone, the hall was prepared anew, fresh food was brought in and Pwyll sat in the seat beside me with all his retinue about us. The feasting continued late into the evening, but before it ended I took Pwyll to my chamber. We spent the night in a blaze of lovemaking until, towards dawn we fell into a blissful sleep, our arms still clasped about each other. But, not long after, a gnarled black hand waved once across my dreams and was gone.

The flame-haired god sinks within the swallowing cauldron. The neck is tied, tightened. The upended bag is now the womb of making. The god within it waiting in darkness. Winter comes. The Lord of Annwn is my consort now. Until the second birthing.

IV

AFTER PWYLL had bestowed Gwawl's bounty on all the suppliants, we left my father's court and travelled together to Dyfed. More feasting and celebration awaited us and I gave gifts to all the noblemen and women of the land.

We reigned together in happiness for two long years, and during that time we hoped a child would come. But in the third year of our reign there was still no child. Fearing I was barren, the men of the land summoned Pwyll and asked him to put me aside and take another woman. But Pwyll held out against them. He asked for another year, and in that year I conceived.

As the festival of Beltain approached, and with it the strong prickings of summer, I felt the child stirring within me, eager to be born. On the Eve of Beltain my womb opened and the child leaped out into the world. He was golden-haired, a child of the sun. When I held him in my arms, joy flowed over me, soothing my body's pain.

That night I wanted to sleep with my babe in my arms. But he was taken and put in a crib beside my bed while my women watched him.

Next morning I woke and reached for him but the crib was empty and there was no one in the room. Then I saw dried blood on my sheet. I called the women. I went towards the door and saw a pile of torn flesh and small bones scattered on the floor. In an agony of fear, I called again.

Then all six women came in as one, their faces grave and unpitying.

'Where is my son?' I cried. 'What is the meaning of this?'

One of the women wrung her hands and began to cry.

'My Lady,' she said, 'do not ask.'

'Do not ask,' echoed the others, and they, too, began weeping. I shook one of them.

'Tell me!' I cried. 'You must tell me!'

Then one of them rolled up her sleeves and showed me red marks beginning to yellow.

'We are all the same,' she answered, 'we are bruised from the blows you gave us when we struggled with you.'

'You were too strong for us,' wailed another.

'You destroyed him!' shouted a third.

'You killed him yourself!' they all cried together. 'Don't blame us. There was nothing we could do!'

I saw that they were frightened.

'You poor souls,' I said, 'as the gods are my witness I know your accusations are false.'

I looked round their faces, trying to catch their eyes, but they all looked away.

'Tell me what happened,' I said. 'If you fear for your lives, I promise to protect you. Only you must tell me the truth.'

'As the gods themselves will bear witness,' answered the oldest woman, 'we will not put ourselves in the wrong in this.'

'You poor souls,' I said again, 'you will come to no harm if you tell the truth.'

I pleaded with them then. Over and over again I begged them to tell me what had happened, to speak the truth. Nevertheless the women stuck to their tale.

After they left me, I fell back on the bed as the shuddering of my body took hold. A distant voice screamed in my head that my son could not have gone. It was impossible. I could still feel him, lying in the ache of my arm. When I opened my eyes I saw Pwyll and some men of the court standing over me. I saw his mouth moving and some of his men's mouths, but I was unable to hear them. One was lifting up a tiny skull. It had a barely-formed snout. In my fevered state, I remember thinking it could have come from the litter of a deer.

Some days later, Pwyll came to me and held me gently. He told me that the chief men of the land had come to him and demanded that he put me away. It was because of the terrible crime that the women swore I had committed. Tears were flowing down my face.

'But I told them,' he said, 'that they had no right to demand that. I told them they could only insist I put you away if you were barren.'

He held me tighter and spoke into my neck.

'I told them that because you were not barren I would not put you away.'

He held me for a long time, and then he released me and looked into my face.

'But,' he said quietly,' I had to promise them you would do penance for the crime.'

Next day I summoned my wise men and advisers and we weighed the merits of my case. Unless I could get the women to confess what I was sure had happened – that they had fallen asleep and the child had disappeared, perhaps been stolen, I had to undertake my penance. I thought of their faces, of the raw terror that had made them lie to me, that had made them kill a deer's pups and blame me for their negligence, and I knew I had no choice but to undergo the penance. But something in me was broken with the grief. Something in me could no longer put up a fight. Something in me was willing to bear humiliation.

I am bowed down, a pale beast of burden. I wait by the mounting-block at the foot of the hill. All who have business at the palace come by me. I tell them my tale. I am the slayer of my child. I have told it so many times I almost begin to believe it. I killed my child. I fought off the nursing women and I killed him. He is dead because of me. I tossed his bones on the floor. I held him one sweet day and then I killed him. I am a mother who lost her child through her own evil.

Somehow it helps me with my grief. It is a lay, a dirge for the dead. I sing my
song for all women, women who carry a phantom babe within their arm,
whose breasts weep milk, whose child is snatched away by the hand of fate.

Then I take them on my back and carry them up to the palace.

V

AFTER FOUR years the grief in me was still strong. And there were yet
another three years left of my penance. My back ached constantly with
the effort of carrying each man, woman or child who came visiting, up
the hill to the palace. I was beaten by the weather, my face was red, my
hands rough. Hour after hour in hurling rain, harsh wind or burning
sunlight, I stayed at my post. I was a strong woman now.

Then one day a small party approached the palace. They had
come from Gwent Is-Coed. The chief of that place was Teyrnon Twryf
Liant. He was lord of Gwent and I knew how highly Pwyll regarded
him, for Teyrnon had served him at court in former times.

I greeted Teyrnon, his son and two companions.

'Chieftain,' I called out. 'Do not go further, for I will bear each
one of you on my back up to the castle.'

The four of them stood there, unmoving. As I began to tell
them my tale they cut me short. Teyrnon said:
'Lady, I do not think any of us will agree to ride on your back.'

A boyish voice piped up:
'Let those who would climb on your back do so. I, for one,
will not.'

'Nor', said his father, 'shall we.'

Then they walked up the hill.

When I had finished my penance for the day I washed myself
and prepared to dine in the Great Hall. I guessed that tonight there
would be a special feast to mark Teyrnon's unexpected visit.

At the feast Teyrnon sat between Pwyll and myself, and his son sat between his two companions. After the first course, when the time came for conversation, Teyrnon turned to Pwyll.

'I have a story to tell you,' he said, 'and it is one of great wonder.'

His face was glowing with the excitement of the tale and something about his eagerness set my heart beating.

'You may know,' he said, 'that I have a mare in my house. It is famous throughout Gwent, for there is hardly a handsomer beast in the country. What is less well known is that she foals each year on Beltain Eve. What happens to the foal no one knows, for come morning it can never be found.

'Now', said Teyrnon, and he narrowed his eyes, 'I have always bowed to this circumstance. For I have always had respect for the magic of it. The veil between the worlds is raised at Beltain, as we all know, and what happens then and what is exchanged between the worlds, is not for us to ask. But four years ago I determined to save the foal if I could. I brought it into the stable, took up my weapons and set watch over it. Come midnight the mare gave birth. The birth was swift. The foal tumbled from her and stood up immediately, as strong as if it were already a few days old. I, too, stood up to admire it but, as I did so, there came a great clamour and commotion outside the stable. Before I could do anything a huge arm was thrust through the window and a clawed hand snatched up the foal. I had my sword in my hand, so I hacked at the arm and cut it off at the elbow. There was a crash outside and a great scream while the arm and the colt fell together back into the stable. I rushed out, but the night was black as the bottom of a pit and nothing could be seen, not the glint of my sword, nor even the smoke of my breath. I ran into the darkness following the retreating clamour but was unable to pursue it. Then I remembered I had left the door to the stable open. I ran back to check the colt, but when I reached the stable I saw a strange thing. There, in the doorway was a babe, dropped in the commotion. I gathered it up in my arms and took it into my wife. The child was wrapped in a cloak of silk brocade. The child was strong, like the foal, though it, too, seemed newly birthed.'

Teyrnon turned and looked at me. My face was white. Silently I willed him to go on with his story.

'What you may not know,' he said, 'is that my wife and I are childless. So you will understand that we had no hesitation in accepting this child from the Otherworld, this boy with the yellow hair who tumbled into our stable on Beltain Eve. The child grew prodigiously in the first year and was walking well before the year was out. By the second year the boy had the look of a six-year-old child. By the fourth year, still being advanced for his age, we gave him the colt that was born alongside him.'

Teyrnon turned to me again. The water was gathering in my eyes.

'And then we heard of your plight, Rhiannon,' he said. And we looked at the boy.'

He paused while all the court regarded the sturdy son that had followed him into the court and who now sat between his two companions, his head held high. All saw the great resemblance he had to Pwyll.

'Lady, look. There is your son!' said Teyrnon. 'It was a lie that was told against you.'

He stood up.

'And now I don't think there is anyone here in this court who will deny that the boy is Pwyll's son,' he cried.

A great roar of assent like a huge and mounting wave came from all those at the feast.

'Oh, if this is true,' I breathed, as the room began to tumble round me in a blur of fluttering lights. 'By all the gods,' I said, while all eyes looked at me. 'If this is true then all my pain and care is gone!'

I rose but could not feel my limbs. I sat again and the boy came towards me.

'That is a good name, his mother has given him'. It was Pandarus speaking, one of the chieftains of Dyfed.

'Pryderi, son of Pwyll, Lord of Annwyn.'

By now the boy was in my arms. My face was in his golden hair. I was weeping yet faint with the wonder of it. Should he be called Pryderi? Pryderi meant 'care', 'trouble'.

After a while I said:

'What if the child's own name suits him better?'

'What is his name?' Pandarus asked Teyrnon.

'We called him Gwri Golden Hair because of the hair that danced in peaks upon his head,' he replied.

'Pryderi should be his name,' said Pandarus decisively.

'It is the name his mother spoke when she heard the news of him.'

It was Pwyll who said these words. He looked at me and, as he did so, the world turned for me. The fruits and bounty of the cauldron flowed again. I knew that not only was my son restored, but with him my honour, my people, my land. Also the ancient power, the timeless power of the Mother - the power to name her son.

Rhiannon 2

Vengeance can be a long time in the coming. Long after I thought I was safe, long after Pwyll died and my son Pryderi had grown and married and gone to war with Bran and then come back, it finally came upon me.....

OF THOSE seven who returned from the war with Erin, Pryderi was one. He came home a sadder man with his new comrade, Manawydan. Manawydan was Bran and Branwen's brother, all of them children of the sea god Llyr. As soon as I set eyes on him I knew that Manawydan was inscrutable. His eyes were deep as oceans, and he kept his own counsel. I thought perhaps he was engendering a new wisdom. I also saw how my son was drawn to him. More than that, when he introduced me to his new friend, Pryderi's eyes were dancing.

Manawydan looked at me, then he smiled and flashed a glance at Pryderi. When we sat at dinner Manawydan sat beside me. We conversed with each other, and I remember there was eagerness in his conversation and that we laughed gently together. Suddenly he shot another look at Pryderi.

'Pryderi, I accept your offer', he said.

Pryderi grinned delightedly.

'What offer is that?' I asked.

'Mother', said Pryderi, 'I have done a bold thing. I have offered you as wife to Manawydan.'

In the astonished hush that followed, they both regarded me with baited breath.

I think my heart stopped in that moment – or perhaps it was time itself that stopped. And in that moment I felt as if I was lifted off my feet

*and was floating in the spaces of Manawydan's eyes. I thought I could even
hear his heart beating beside me as I turned in unknown worlds, tasting my
future. How long I lingered in this timeless place I will never know —
perhaps it was only an instant, a brief flash as I shifted from one state to
another. For, as suddenly as I had spun into other worlds, I returned to
myself. I breathed again, and all breathed with me.*

'I accept gladly.' I said.

'And so do I!' said Manawydan.

That was all it took. And, after that, the homecoming feast
became a bridal celebration.

That night I led my new young husband to my chamber. I
remember how he held me while I gazed into the green depths of his
eyes. I thought then how he was nothing like Pwyll, Gwawl, or indeed
any other suitor I had ever had. He kissed me with a deep and surprising
passion and said that my conversation and my wit were as compelling
as my beauty. I said that my beauty was perhaps waning a little but I
hoped my wisdom remained sharp. He laughed at that and kissed me
again. Then he lay with me.

This was a man who was a stranger to me, a man I had yet to
know. He seemed fearless, possessed of a strange strength, yet he lacked
the quick anger, the battle-mad bravado of other men. 'One of the
Three Ungrasping Chieftains' Pryderi had called him. This was
something to wonder at.

Next day the wedding feast continued. Pryderi told me he had
partly urged the marriage because he wanted Manawydan to have land
now that his throne had been usurped. This was an extraordinary offer
and we all knew it. For, under the new ways, Pryderi was giving away
his own land to Manawydan. I glanced at Cygfa, Pryderi's wife, to see
how she had taken this, but she kept her head down and showed
no reaction.

Then Pryderi made another extraordinary announcement:

'I have decided to leave the feast early and go to London to give homage to Caswallawn' ' he said.

His words were met with an astonished silence for, though Caswallawn was high King, it was through magic and treachery that he had come to power. At last I spoke into the silence:

'Caswallawn is in Kent,' I said quietly. 'Why not wait until he comes nearer and then go and pay him homage.'

The plan was agreed and we continued feasting together. I could see Cygfa was pleased with my advice, as she wanted to keep Pryderi with us.

After we had finished our celebrations, the four of us made a tour of Dyfed. Manawydan looked at its heathered fields, its silver rivers and tumbling meadows, its sharp-sided mountains and clinging valleys, and his mind filled with childhood memories. Often he wept for Bran and his sister Branwen and often he sighed at the thought of Caswallawn, the new High King, the savage magician who had stolen amongst the chiefs of our island wearing his cloak of invisibility, and who had killed all seven of them – Bran's guardians, and then seized the throne. But neither Manawydan nor Pryderi talked of an uprising. It was as if the horrors of the war in Erin, the great toll of death and the wasted land had taken the fight out of them.

For my part, I kept my counsel and watched them. I knew that kings might come and go, and wars might yet be waged, but now the power of the Mother was gone, for the great cauldron was broken, and the like of it could only be found in the Otherworld.

Perhaps this thought was at the back of all our minds. Perhaps this was why, after Pryderi returned from paying homage to Caswallawn at Oxford, we behaved so rashly and flirted so outrageously with the powers of the Otherworld....

It was a few nights after Pryderi's return, towards the end of a new feast, that we all four got up and, taking a company with us, went to climb the Mound of Arberth. Like Pwyll before us, we knew this was a portal to the Otherworld. We knew we could expect either a terrible blow or a wondrous marvel. We knew the risk of it and yet we went.

When we reached the top of the mound, we sat and waited. We waited until the sun went down and dampness rose from the earth. Then far groans of thunder came to our ears. Faint at first, it soon rolled upon us with a great roaring so that we clutched our ears. It roared over us like a huge-winged dragon and, as it passed, a thick smoke blew in our faces and hid each one of us from the other. As the heavy mist began pulling apart it was speared with shafts of harsh white light. The light grew until it blanched every part of the country around us. In its glare we first saw the emptiness. The fields were stripped of horses and cattle, the pastures were bare of sheep. The smoke was stopped in the chimneys of the huts and houses, and no man could be seen in the farmsteads. We looked at each other and realised that our company had also disappeared and that only the four of us remained.

'Alas! cried Manawydan, 'where are our companions?'

As we stood together dazed with shock, he said:

'Let us go and see what has happened to the rest of the court?'

We descended the mound and went into the great hall. The feast was still spread out, but no one sat at table. We went through to the kitchens and mead cellars. No on was tending the pots. We went through the chambers. Each was empty.

A spell had been cast over the land, emptying the seven cantrevs of Dyfed of all human life and livestock. All that remained were ourselves and the wild animals.

At first, believing the magic would not last forever, we contented ourselves with these conditions. The four of us were very close, so close we were almost as one. Indeed, we were never happier than in each other's company. So, while the stores of food held out, we feasted together and roamed the lands around the court. When we needed fresh supplies we fished or hunted for game, and afterwards prepared our own food.

In this way two years passed.

Yet we were under enchantment. For time flowed strangely in the empty land beyond the mist. After two years – or perhaps a blink of time only, we decided to leave Dyfed and journey into Loegres. Here there had been no emptying of the land. There were people and farmsteads, villages and trade. Soon after we arrived in Hereford, Manawydan decided to humble himself and take up a craft. He began making saddles for horses and we helped him. The saddles he made had blue pommels, for he enamelled them in azure, bright and glittering as birds' wings. His skill was rare, his saddles beautiful beyond description. He made them for those who wished to ride in style, those who would tame and bridle their horses, those that would sit up straight as a spear and be admired. His saddles, I knew, were of a rare and noble quality but, all the same, I myself would rather bend to my mare's wildness, grip her flanks with my bare legs, goad her with my naked feet, and feel that she and I were one.

Time passed while Manawydan continued making saddles to tame the horses. A year turned - or perhaps an age. Then, when the other traders saw they were losing business to Manawydan's skill, they banded together and threatened us. Pryderi would have fought them, but Manawydan held up his hand while the points of wisdom glittered in the oceans of his eyes.

'It is better for us,' he said, 'to leave now and journey to another town and make another living.'

And so we found ourselves in another town, another year and, for all we knew, another age. This time Manawydan made shields for men to carry with them on their horses. Again, he finished them with blue enamel, bright as birds' wings. Proudly the men carried the shields to war. Proudly they sat upon their horses and urged them onto the battlefields. Tournaments were fought then, in which the colours of Manawydan's shields blazed on the fields. No man of noble birth would sport a shield of lesser workmanship. Again the people of the town lost trade and our lives were threatened. Again Pryderi would have fought with them, but Manawydan persuaded him against such action, and made us journey on.

We were harried into a third town, a third age it may have been, a third craft. This time Manawydan humbled himself to work with leather. Cygfa said he stooped too low for a king's son. But Manawydan looked at her in that piercing way he had, and she said no more. Manawydan bought only the softest and the stoutest leather, he bought buckles and had them gilded by the best goldsmiths in the town. His shoes were the lightest yet most stout and beautifully crafted to be found – and for that he was later called One of the Three Gold Shoemakers. But again, as had happened before, the shoemakers of the town began to lose their trade, and our lives were once more threatened.

So, at last, we journeyed back to Dyfed, our enchanted homeland and entered once more our deserted palace at Arberth. There lay the court as we had left it, except that weeds had seized it and some stone had crumbled. Still no breath of human life disturbed its emptiness.

We made a fire in the middle of the Great Hall and in its flames we watched each other's faces. As yet no difficulty had come between the four of us. We still felt we were everything to each other.

We cleared and reclaimed our palace, and another year passed while we chased small game and fed ourselves by roasting the wild creatures on the fire. This time we had animals to help us, for we had brought dogs back with us for hunting. But it was mostly the two men, Manawydan and Pryderi who went out to hunt while Cygfa and I stayed behind.

Then one strange morning in that wild and empty land the two men got up early as usual and left the court. Everything was about to change again, a new enchantment was nearby but they did not know it. They were gone all day, but that was nothing new. Except that in the evening Manawydan came back home alone.

'Where is Pryderi?' I asked him.

Manawydan shook his head. He did not look into my eyes.

'Where is he?' I asked again.

Manawydan spread his hands.

'I don't know," he said simply. Then he told us his tale.

'We left the court this morning, as you know,' he said 'and our hounds ran on ahead to a small copse. We saw them enter it, then run out again. They were howling and shivering, their hair rising up like stalks of corn. Pryderi was all for going into the copse to see what was there. But as we went towards it, a wild boar, glowing white as if it were at the edge of Annwn itself, burst out of it. Urged by our cries, the hounds pursued it. But it behaved strangely. It stood at bay against the dogs until we drew near, then it ran on, as if it were trying to lead us somewhere. And lead us it did. Straight up the Mound of Arberth. And there, on its summit we came upon a tall fortress, the like of which had never been there before. The boar and the hounds ran inside and after that there was silence. The animals never came out again, nor did we hear the hounds give a single bark.'

Manawydan looked at us and shadows were in his eyes.

'Pryderi was all for going into the castle to find out what had happened to our dogs. But I knew it was a portal of magic. I told him this castle had never been here before and that he should not go inside.'

He looked at me and tears were in his eyes.

'I counselled him strongly. I warned him not to go in,' he said, 'but he wouldn't listen.

'I will not give up my dogs!' he shouted and went into the castle. I waited outside. I waited for him all day but, like the boar and the hounds before him, he never came out.'

I looked at Manawydan and, at that moment, I hated him. The love of my child rose like a tremor through my body. I cried out:

'In the name of all the gods, how could you have left him! How could you have been so bad a companion and lost such a good one?'

Then, before he could stop me, I started running towards the mound in the falling darkness.

When I came near the top of it, I could see the fortress plainly and the gateway to it standing open. I ran through the gateway and on into the castle. Then I stopped and gasped at the sight before me. Ahead of me, in the middle of the floor, was a fountain rising up and, surrounding it, a step of marble. On the fountain's edge was a golden bowl of exquisite crafting. Above it were four chains that rose into the air so that the bowl seemed to be hanging from the sky. Holding the bowl in his two hands was Pryderi, his face reflecting gold from its light.

I called out:

'My lord, what are you doing here?'

But my voice died in the empty fort and he gave me no reply. Then I saw he was still as a statue, unmoving. I ran up to him and, before I could touch him, it was as if the crafted signs upon the bowl rose and danced in the air before me. I stooped down and laid my hands beside his on its dazzling rim.

And now, like Pryderi, I am bound to the bowl, my hands stuck tight to its rim, my feet immobile on the marble slab. But the bowl is moving. The rim is turning beneath our hands. We can neither move our heads nor look into each other's eyes. We cannot speak. A pall of darkness falls on us. A thunderous roar sounds overhead, blaring our ears. Time stops, or passes, we are whirled away. Time retreats, goes backwards. Our second blow. My son and I returned to penance. The cauldron with the captured Goddess whirls into the Otherworld. Without the magic bowl, the land lies empty.

I do not know how long we remained in this state, chained to this empty place, held in this stuck time, nor do I know how long we would have stayed there. But I do know that it was Manawydan who got us back. Manawydan, who had the wit not to enter the *caer*. Manawydan who waited and watched, then seized his opportunity and formed a plan. But it took him a long time.

At first, after we were gone he took Cygfa back to the realm of Loegres and became a Golden Shoemaker as before. Then, when the men rose up against him, he brought seed from Loegres and travelled back to Dyfed to harvest it. He tilled the soil and waited for the crop to grow. And the land answered him. Up sprang three meadowsful of wheat ears, white-gold as the Lammas' sun. While they waited for the harvesting Manawydan and Cygfa fished and hunted and bagged the combs of bees as before. Although they were the only two in the whole of Dyfed, Manawydan laid no finger on Cygfa. They slept apart and waited only for their crop to ripen.

But when the morning of the first day of harvest came, they found the first meadow stripped clean by an unseen hand. Only the bare stalks stood up broken against the sky. On the morning of the second day they found the second field as bare and broken as the first.

'This is the work of whoever started the enchantment,' Manawydan thought to himself. 'Whatever power laid the land waste is now ruining my crop.'

He said to Cygfa:

'I will keep watch tonight and find out who is doing this.'

Then he lay in wait and watched over the third croft.

Midnight came and with it a loud rustling like a strong wind tearing through the ears of wheat. In the wide light of the moon, he saw a host of gleaming white mice swarming through the field. Each had climbed an ear and was biting through its stalk. In great anger, Manawydan ran amongst the crop, trying to catch them, but the mice darted from his grasp. Then he saw a mouse that was heavier than the rest and less swift. He caught it by the tail, swung it in the air and dropped it in his glove. Then he tied up the glove with a cord.

He returned to the castle and hung the glove from a peg.

'What have you got there?' asked Cygfa.

'A thief' he replied, 'And I will hang it tomorrow.'

Then he told her the story of his nightly vigil.

'And if I had caught all the mice,' he added, 'I would hang every one of them!'

'My lord,' said Cygfa, 'that is not surprising! And yet I think you stoop too low in this. It is not right that a man of your rank and dignity should be hanging such a creature. Why don't you let it go?'

'If I knew of any reason in the world why I should, I would do so,' answered Manawydan. 'But as none appears to me, I will continue with my plan to kill it.'

After that it was the wit of Manawydan that took the mouse to the top of the Mound of Arberth. It was the wisdom of Manawydan that planted the two forks in the top of the mound and made as if to start the hanging. It was the perception of Manawydan that waited until he saw a figure coming towards him. And that was the first sighting of a man in the whole of Dyfed for seven years, except for the four of us that used to live together.

The figure that came towards him was a clerk wearing threadbare clothes, and peddling songs from Loegres. When he saw the noose around the mouse's neck, the clerk offered him alms for its release but Manawydan refused to be bribed, and the clerk went away disappointed. Then a priest came and offered him gold coins for the creature's release, but again Manawydan refused to be bribed and continued with his task.

A third figure came after that, a proud and stately bishop with a company of men about him. He offered him even more gold for the safety of the mouse. Still Manawydan held his course. The bishop offered him the company's horses and all their baggage. By now Manawydan had the string about the mouse's neck and was about to let it drop.

'Then what is your price for freeing her?' asked the bishop quickly.

'The return of Rhiannon and Pryderi,' Manawydan replied.

'You shall have that.'

'Yet that is not enough,' said Manawydan.

'What else do you want?'

'The enchantment to be lifted from the land.'

'You shall have that.'

'Even that is that enough' said Manawydan, 'I want to know who the mouse is.'

The bishop sighed.

'Very well,' he answered heavily. 'I shall tell you everything. I am Llywd, son of Kil Coed, and the mouse with the noose about its neck is my wife, enchanted like my army, into a plague of mice intending to lay waste your crop. And it is because she is bearing my child that you were able to catch her. But if you want to know why both my war-band and then my wife and the ladies of the court persuaded me to transform them into mice, it was to avenge my cousin Gwawl that we plotted all this.'

After that it was Manawydan's wisdom that ended the bargaining by making the bishop swear to make no further spells and take no further vengeance – neither on me, nor on my son, nor on himself.

A strange man, I had thought, was Manawydan. The 'Ungrasping Chieftain' - a man of fearlessness, of strength. A king's son who would not prove himself with rash acts of boldness. A man who could not be cowed, or moved by jeers or bribery. A man who was shrewd enough to hold fast against the dark magician and bring about the freeing of the land.

When he had brought back my son and me from the dark and nameless place, we still had the tokens of captivity hanging on us. As Manawydan lifted the ass's collar from my neck, I looked into the oceans of his eyes. And, as I looked, the bargained pledge took hold, the halls and houses shifted to their former state, the vanished people came again into their halls and huts, the land became young, the crops sprang up across the fields and crofts, the herds of sheep and cows again grazed quietly upon the meadows.

And now my three birds fly about my head, singing their songs of promise from the threshold of the Otherworld. Far and near. Near and far. Now, too, my love lies with me in the land's embrace – restored, replenished. Holding me with his wondrous eyes, his wit, his shrewdness.

Ah, could all such men of wisdom bring the Goddess home!

CRONE
GODDESSES

CRONE

IN HER Crone aspect, the Goddess finds herself in the darkness, having been defeated by humiliation and death. Yet in this place she discovers new powers. There are riches here, the hidden secrets of new life. At this time the Goddess becomes wise-woman and prophetess. It is now her role to initiate the hero into these spiritual mysteries. So, in these tales, we see her become strong and fearless. She is ready to test the hero for the tasks of kingship, on the battlefield or in the face of death itself. And, though she has been much feared and maligned in this role, those who understand her know that after the time of challenge comes rebirth.

The voice of the Crone comes out of the shadow.
It is the voice of wisdom, the voice of the seer –
the Initiator into Mysteries.

It is the voice that knows the secrets of death,
the voice that men most fear,
the voice they have almost silenced.

For it is the voice of vision
and the powers of the unseen,
the voice of the Challenger.

THE MORRIGAN 1

THE PAPS of the Morrigan are two rounded hills beside the River Boyne. Thus Lough Neagh is my grey eye, the slope of Ben Bulben my nose, the valley beneath Sligo Bay my slippery thighs, and the River Unius the water running from my body's hollows.

But I was not lying across Erin, I was standing astride the Unius making the waters when the Dagda first came to me. Huge as the earth was he. Covering the land he penetrated the impenetrable places, the shivering gorges, the dark valleys, the desolate ravines.

My hair was hanging in nine loosed flame-red tresses, numbered for the nine-fold goddess, when he came. My head stood high above the land, high as the burning trails of the retreating sun. My right foot was bare and rested above the water on Loscuinn, my left was on Allod Echae. The Dagda played to me on the Harp of the Seasons. Its sound was as the waters of the world forever flowing.

Then I, the Great Goddess of the land with my breasts and my flame-licked hair and my wet thighs raised the huge club of the Great God - the club that furrows the earth, the club that kills with its blunt end and, with the other, sows its seed, and let him enter me.

A long time after we were joined, the sun plunged below the earth's great bowl and sank in blackness. Yet still the Great God was not spent.

I am the Goddess of Death. I am also *Mor Rigan*, the Great Queen, Sovereign of the Land and Goddess of Rebirth. The Dagda is my consort. We are well matched.

The Dagda came to me on the Eve of Samhain. And now all through the darkness and the sleep-time of the land his seed will lie hidden in the cauldron of my womb.

After we parted, the seer's sight came upon me. My eyes

reached inwards to my vision. I saw the Old Ones from Beneath the Sea, the Fomorians, half-formed holders of the ancient powers. I saw them gathering on the plain, the lords of death and prophecy, shape-changers to a man. Fair one moment, and the next misshapen. For they are the black-skinned ones, the one-eyed, one-armed, one-legged ones. And any who would curse in earnest must call upon their unity of purpose – the singleness of eye and limb.

In my Cailleach form I draw upon their powers. My legs turn black, one eye squints, one leg is crippled. My mouth enlarges. It is like the mouth of the Old Ones with three full rows of teeth.

I am before all time. Dark and Light are alike to me.

I told the Dagda the Fomorians would come ashore at Mag Scetne and gather there for battle. I told him to summon the men of art, the skilled ones of the Tuatha de Danaan, and bring them to meet me at the ford of my river. I said I would go onto the Plain of Scetne and bring down Indech, the Fomorian king. I would cast a terror on him that would strip his heart and kidneys of blood and courage. Then I would bring two handfuls of his blood to the army waiting at the ford. This I would do for him, for he is the Great God and he honours me.

The thing happened as I decreed. The Fomorians gathered at Mag Scetne. I saw them as a huddled host, a black mass on the plain. I called my sisters, Badbh and Nemain. Together we flew as ragged crows about the battlefield. Shrieking above the metalled heads we called the phantom troops – the black spirits of the air, the creatures of the night, the wild-eyed hags, the shades, the demons. Our unseen army laid its fearful pall upon the battlefield and drained the courage of the Fomorians. But we ourselves raised battle lust among the Tuatha, fevering their blood, stirring them to the frenzy of the kill, firing them with battle madness, like the sweet frenzy of begetting life.

When the fever was spent, in the limb-strewn field, among the ruin of the weapons and the twisted corpses, the druids of the Tuatha went like white birds about the field, their thick robes drinking the half-dried blood. And there they lifted their staffs, intoned their magic, and bound the remnant of the Fomorian army with their curses and enchantments.

Then I, the Great Queen of the Land of Erin in my own form went up to the high places and shouted the victory from the mountains so that the hills, the loughs and rivers all heard the news, so that even the *sidhe*, the spirit hosts of all the woods and places of the earth would listen. For the renewing of the land touched fire to my belly, the ecstasy of peace after the intoxication of battle. As I went among the places of the land, the people asked me: 'Have you a tale to tell?'

This was my answer:

> I proclaim peace, peace that stretches to the sky
> that lies upon the earth under the sky.
> I call up strength in every man and woman
> that their cup will brim with fullness of sweet honey
> that honour be enough,
> That summer shall lay itself over winter …
> that the trees of the woods shall be thick
> with curling pointed crowns – the antlers of stags.
> That all destruction end.

> Instead that there be
> branches hanging to the ground with yield,
> heaviness of nuts in season,
> overflowing nature, wealth of all mankind,
> fuel for fire, and leaping flames for warmth.
> That the wisdom of the Salmon be considered victory,
> and the Otherworldly Boyne shall be as home.
> New growth, renewal of the land –
> a land secure, its power expressed in sacred word.

> Power to the bright woods,
> Peace ascending to the sky
> Be nine times blessed
> To all eternity.

But after emptying my heart and blessing the land, I saw far off its evil. And so I made a warning and a lament that one day I would not see a world that would be dear to me. For I saw a time when there would be lack of valour in the young and lack of wisdom in the old, when deception of the people and meaningless seduction would overtake the earth. I saw a time when summer would be without vegetation, cattle without milk, woods without yield, and sea without fish.

And I, the Morrigu, raised this lament and made this prophecy, but no man wished to hear me.

THE MORRIGAN 2

THE CRY I make is the harsh scream of the Cailleach. It rattles the stars in their sockets and sets the moon's teeth on edge. I wield it like a jagged blade, slitting the heavens, cracking the shell of the sky with a silver shriek like lightning. Then I wait. I wait for the thundering answer of a man, a king, a god.
I wait.

I was emptying my cry into the night as I screeched down from the north towards Dun Innid. I was standing in my chariot, my red hair like a flung web, my two eyes glittering, opals of unfallen sweat on my ash-pale skin. My cloak that had stretched behind me like a dragon's wing hung lifeless between the chariot wheels as I halted at Ath da Ferta.

My great scream and the rattle of my bone-poled chariot brought two men – Lugaid the charioteer and Cuchulainn, his warrior cargo. We met, chariot to chariot, beside the ford. Laig with his bronze headband holding back his spilling mass of hair, his muscle-fronded arms so deft with whip and harness, Cuculainn dishevelled, his armour half-buckled over his night tunic – so quickly had he been roused at deep of night by my call.

The one red horse that drew my chariot was of the Fomorian type. It had one foot and the chariot pole was thrust through its head, coming out mid-brow. Beside my horse was a cow herded by a giant of a man with a two-pronged hazel staff.

Cuchulainn looked only at the man.

'The cow does not like you driving it!' he said.

'It is not your cow,' I answered haughtily, 'nor do I think she belongs to any friend or fellow countryman of yours.'

'The cows of Ulster are my concern.' Cuchulainn answered.

'And do you now have rule over the cows?' I said drily. 'You aim too high Cuchulainn!'

Still he had not looked at me. His eyes were on the man beside me.

He said to himself, as if wondering aloud:

'Why is the woman answering me instead of the man?'

'It is not the man you addressed.' I replied.

'It is, but you answered for him.'

'In that case I will tell you his name,' I said acidly. 'He-is-the-wind-that-shrills-through-the-night.' I said this both to mock him and to speak riddles.

'His name is indeed extraordinary!' replied Cuchulainn. He turned to me at last, and said reluctantly:

'If he will not answer, then I suppose you may answer for him. What is your own name?'

Before I could open my mouth, the man spoke for me, carrying on the game.

'The woman's name,' he said, 'is Slight-mouthed, fair-finished, light-tressed, tight-pointed one of great clamour!'

'Do you take me for a fool?' shouted Cuchulainn and, propelled by sudden rage, he made his salmon leap through the air, landing with his feet astride my shoulders and his spear pressed to the crown of my head.

I sat unmoving.

'Don't threaten me with your pointed toys!' I said.

'Then tell me your proper name!' snarled Cuchulainn.

'Get down then!' I snapped, 'If you must know, I am a female bard and this man is Daire mac Fiachna of Cuailnge. As for the cow, it is the fee for a master poem.'

There was disbelief and contempt on Cuchulainn's face. He still had his spear poised above my head.

'Tell me the poem!' he demanded.

'Only if you stop threatening me!'

Then he climbed down from my chariot and stood between its poles.

I summoned my seer's powers. With a harsh voice I sang a foretelling of the slaughter of the Cattle Raid, the *Tain Bo Cuailnge*. I sang of the hero's prowess and the waste of war. It was a satire.

As soon as I had finished Cuchulainn sprang at me again. But this time, as he sprang into the air we all vanished in the black of night – the chariot, the man, the horse, myself, even the cow.

And now I was a raven on the branch beside him, cawing over him as he landed ignominiously on the loamy turf.

'You are indeed a dangerous and magical woman,' he said. 'A sorceress.'

My eyes flickered.

'As for this place,' I said, 'it has become a place of evil. Grellech Dulluid will be its name now.'

'If I had known it was you,' said Cuchulainn, 'we would not have parted in this way.'

'What you have done,' I said, 'will bring evil on you.'

'You cannot hurt me!' said Cuchulainn.

'I wouldn't be so sure,' I replied. 'For it is I who guard your death and will continue to do so.'

Then I made a second prophecy, this time concerning his death.

'The cow you saw with me, ' I said, 'is a heifer I brought from the mound of the *sidhe* in Cruachan. She is to breed by the Brown Bull, the Donn of Cuailnge. When her calf is one year old your life will end.'

I added quietly:

'But first there will be the Cattle Raid!'

Undaunted, Cuchulainn replied:

'Then I will become famous through this Cattle Raid. I shall do great and mighty deeds, I shall hew down warriors, I shall be foremost in battles. Also,' he added, looking boldly up at me. 'I shall survive the Raid.'

'I would be less boastful if I were you!' I said sharply. 'For you will come against men who are as skilled, as brave and as mighty as yourself. And, indeed, I may even come against you myself!'

Cuchulainn looked at me with contempt.

'Very well! I shall come as an eel in the ford and coil about your ankle, to trip you,' I said sharply.

'As to that,' Cuchulainn retorted, 'I will crush you against the stones of the river and you will not know peace until you leave me.'

'In that case,' I said, ' I will change into a grey wolf and take the strength from your right hand.'

'Then I will burst your eye with my spear until I drive you off,' shouted Cuchulainn, the hairs on his head rising in his anger.

'If so,' I returned drily, 'I shall change into a white cow with two red ears and lead a hundred such cows to trample you in the ford!'

'Ha! Then I shall break your foreleg with a sling stone and force you to turn aside!' returned Cuchulainn, his face already half distorted by his battle-warp.

With our angry words still hanging in the air, he got into his chariot and made Laeg drive him back to Muirthemne.

......

I came once more to Cuchulainn in my flame-haired form. It was during the great war of the *Tain*, the Cattle-Raid of Cuailnge. I was in my high-sided chariot, my red hair flickering on my shoulders, bright against the dusk of the day. I told him I was the daughter of King Buan. I stepped down from my chariot and offered him riches and cattle. Then I breathed my flame into his mouth.

My flame is the sweetest pleasure known to man. It thrills his blood, it flares his pupils, it lifts the hairs upon his back, it flickers tongues of heat about his body, it strokes his limbs, it shafts into his loins. If he had joined with me the Hound of Ulster could have had the land itself, the fertile plains, the stretched peaks of the mountains, the heaving hills, the damp and hidden valleys, the sinewed rivers, the jewelled mines, the tumbled gorges.

But instead Cuchulainn threw me from him with an oath. 'I have not come here for the backside of a woman!' he sneered.

I left him then. But I had discovered enough. His heart lay not in the love of the land. It was in the joy of blood and battle, the delight of overcoming – kings, warriors, enemies, and the powers of women.

Now I only see death and make my prophesies. No one pushes through my darkness into life. And so my body, whether it be fair or foul, lies locked in winter…

THE MORRIGAN 3

THE MELODY of the hole-headed lute that Cruaiphtine the harper played today still lingers. Its notes hang like smoke. The lament haunts the sweet air.

I kneel at the ford. Beneath the tumbling water the cushions and harnesses of the chariot slip and squeak through my fingers. The enamelled mounts are bellied with clotted blood, the ash wheel-spokes woven with entrails. With my long fingers I unplait the twisted guts.

A voice says: 'What that woman is doing is horrible.'

I lift my fingers from the red water. They are white, unspotted. No blood drips from my fingers' tips, and no water.

'Go and ask her what she is doing!'

It is the king's voice.

As the messenger approaches me, I rise, I lift one slender knee, I raise a pale arm, close one eye. I chant:

'Hear the groan of the wise raven
Red flames at the door
smoke and burning at the walls
Battle-stones
the graves of warriors
blood reaching to the belts
slaughter of countless hosts,
The king's head lifted
his corpse in its red pool
Fergus weeping.
A grave for the king, a mound
a keening.'

The melody of the hole-headed lute is still in my head. Its mournful tones play about my prophecy.

The messenger turns and heads back to the king. He says:

'It is a prophecy full of evil. Spoken by the Badbh.'

Cormac Connlonges comes to the ford himself. He is Ulster's new king, the exiled son of Conchobor, on his way to take up the throne. He stops when he sees me washing and the red blood flowing.

'Whose harness are you washing?'

'Your harness, Cormac', I reply.

'Your prophecies are grim and full of evil,' he says. Then he turns his back on me and walks away to his chariot.

As he goes my image disappears and, with it, the cushions, the chariot, the king's shield, his harness, together with the wine-bright water. When they have gone, the tide flows again over the mud.

And now a beautiful sun-haired maiden comes, a green cloak around her, a brooch of many jewels on her breast, white bronze sandals on her feet. She approaches Cormac and he welcomes her.

'Are you coming with us?' he asks.

'No.' says the woman. She is gentle, alluring. Water stands in the almonds of her eyes.

She adds softly:

'And I wish that you would not go either. For the ruin of your life awaits you. The lament of the lute – do you remember it - that was your first *geis* breaking.' She looks tenderly into his eyes.

'Do you not know your *geisa* are coming on you and your life is near its end.'

When he remains silent, she looks at him again. This time her eyes are mine. She tells him:

'I shall leave you now and you will not see me again.'

The king lies down then and sleeps. Visions of war are in his dream, of warriors belt-deep in blood, corpses perished in battle and ravens circling.

He wakes and feels the dread upon him, yet continues on his way.

He wants his army to keep marching all the way to Ulster. He wants them not to stop in Cruachan, not even for one more night. For there are tensions between the peoples, debts of honour that cut both ways. But his men say they are safe so long as Fergus is in Cruachan. Besides that, his troops are tired.

They reach Sliab Malonn and decide to stay at the Hostel of Da Choca. It is a Royal Hostel, one of six. It stands at a crossroads like the others. Inside, a pot is always boiling. As soon as they arrive, each man takes up the flesh fork and stabs into the brew. What he brings out is his portion, fair or poor.

Da Choca is a good host and makes the Ulstermen welcome. In the main hall there are no lamps or torches, no light except the fire beneath the cauldron. But the room glows richly. Gold glinting swords, bright flashings of shields, and gold wire decoration all etch strings of light across the walls. Cormac sits against the mid-beam, his head above the rest. There is a light in his eye, his face is long and noble, his chin made narrow by his forked beard and his loosened white-gold hair. The gown of royal purple sits upon his shoulders with the silver brooch that clings to it. The air of the High King is on him and his men glitter about him with their jewels and weapons.

While they rest and dine, I come a third time. But now I am not fair. I lean my shoulder against the doorpost. The whole company can see my blackened skin, my grey hair hanging like a horse-tail down my back, one lame leg buckling beneath me, my mouth enlarged, my left eye rolling, sightless. My cloak is black and holed, the night peers through it.

I give the prophecy of death again. This time all hear it.

I speak in a thin and reedy voice. I am the message of the music of the hole-headed lute, the animals hunted by the king on the hillside of Mag Sainb, the birds that he swam amongst in Loch Lo. I am the voice of the breaking of the *geisa* that were laid on Cormac by the druid Cathbad.

'Nothing,' I say, 'Nothing remains, nothing but limbs torn off, heads taken, corpses stiffening in blood, countless bodies strewn about the clay floor of the hostel.'

After I leave, the company feels the dread upon them like a cloud of ravens fowling and feathering the air about them.

Then new troops from Ulster come and the company is heartened. So easily they forget my warnings.

But in the night the Cruachan army steals round the hostel. Battles have been fought in the new king's name, trust has been broken. Fires are lit silently about the walls. Three times the Ulster warriors sally out, deal slaughter, dowse the fires out with blood. The bodies heap up. In the thin light of morning the blanched faces stare across the plain. Of the Cruachan army of five hundred, only five remain. Of the company of Ulster, only three are left to keen the king and carry the bleak news back to Ulster.

But on the battle site the raw-winged Badbh still swoops and shrieks above the alabaster corpses.

MEDBH

THE FIRST sign that the bull of power was threatened came from my husband, Ailill. It should never have come from him. Daily he saw the sigil on my cloak – the round disc of the moon, bearing the little crescent horn above it. The sign of the Celestial Mother, my own curved body, bearing the crescent horns of youth and springtime.

Though Findabhar, my daughter, has already reached womanhood, my name, 'The Intoxicating One' still serves me. For I am beautiful yet, with my long pale cheeks, my bright mane of yellow hair that brushes my breasts and my two gold birds that hover above my shoulders. And still my thighs can draw men to me. Fergus mac Roth for one – the lustiest warrior of the age, whom only I can satisfy, where seven maids together fail.

But now my bull was leaving …

When I was the age of Findabhar, the whole of Connacht was my inheritance, and how men flocked to woo me! Princes, kings and chiefs of armies, all desperate for my hand. But O how carefully I chose! No man too strong or he would spar with me, nor yet too weak to partner a fearless woman. None too rich to overtop me and yet he must match my generosity, but, above all, no one too jealous of intoxicating power like mine.

'Never,' I told Ailill, when he was chosen, 'never can I keep to one man alone, but I must always have another in the shadows waiting!'

So when he turned his bearded face upon the pillow that fateful morning, and bragged that I was better off in his protection, empowered by all his goods and riches, and lucky to be his wife, I bridled with indignation;

'Let me tell you ' I said, 'before I met you, I was already Queen of Connacht in my own right. Furthermore, I had suitors wooing me from all over Erin. And it was your good fortune that I chose you from among the others. For I had stronger men after me, richer, more jealous, passionate and more powerful.'

'And I'll have you know,' I added, 'that it was for *lack* of such things I chose you!'

But he insisted. Ailill, the consort to my throne, made an outrageous statement:

'Never in the whole of Erin did I hear of a province ruled by a woman except for this one, so I came to take the kingship here. And it was fitting that you, the daughter of the High King of Erin should be my queen.'

Then he waved his wealth and riches in my face, saying that all of Erin knew I could not match them.

I rose, my face pale with anger, biting my lip to redness while my maidens dressed me. Then I struck the main pillar and summoned my servants to the central hall. But Ailill was there before me, lolling amused against another pillar. Eyeing each other, sparring together we gave these orders to our servants: that they should bring out every last stick of each of our possessions – furnishings, jewels, robes, jars, plates and drinking vessels, horses, sheep and cattle, even our servants themselves, and count them.

The counting took days and days. The sheep had to be brought back from the rough hillsides and penned in, the cattle were rounded up, the horses brought in, the boars and pigs collected from the wild. All small items down to the pots and pans and utensils were laid out in two great piles on the green, and then compared and measured. When at last the work was done, they found that our possessions were equally matched in all things but for one – the bull Finbennach Ai, the White-horned, that had been my calf, had left my herd and joined the herd of my husband's cattle. Since then, although my herdsmen had repeatedly tried to bring him back, he had steadfastly refused to return.

As soon as I heard the outcome I went to my chamber and called for Mac Roth, my chief messenger.

'Where in the whole of Erin,' I asked him, 'can a bull be found to equal the Whitehorned?'

'That is easy to answer,' said Mac Roth. 'His equal is Don, the Brown Bull, kept by the chieftain Daire mac Fiachna in the district of Cuailnge in Ulster.'

'Mac Roth,' I said, 'I have an errand for you. Go to Daire and take a party of my servants with you. Say that Queen Medbh would have the loan of Don, the Brown Bull of Cuailnge for one year to match with my husband's bull, Finnbennach. Say to him that at the end of the year I will return the Don with fifty young heifers, and if that is not enough, tell him I will give him a portion of land as good as the one he has already, added to that, a chariot of great worth and, if that is still not sufficient, you may offer him the comfort of my own thighs.'

Within two weeks Mac Roth returned. Without pausing to remove his boots and travelling cloak he swept into the main hall where I was sitting. His face was ambiguous. My tone was dry.

'Well?' I said, 'how did our mission go with Daire?'

'I was obliged to make the full offer, my queen,' he said.

'And?' I asked.

'Daire was jubilant as a boy and bounced on his cushion until he burst the seams.'

I laughed. 'And then?'

'We made an agreement on it and a great feast was prepared for us!'

'What happened then?' I asked.

'My lady, I don't know how to tell you.'

'Go on!' I urged.

Mac Roth sighed. He continued heavily:

'At the feast, the wine was good and there was plenty of it, so that two of our men drank more than their fill. Boasting and bragging they were, and outdoing one another. Then their conversation turned to the King of Ulster – Conchobor. They said there was no better man than he and that if all the Ulster Exiles came back to him there would be no shame in it.'

'Did they, indeed!' I said, bridling.

'But that was not all, my Lady. They began to say how good it was of Daire to give in so easily over the Brown Bull.'

He paused.

'Go on!' I said quietly.

His face twisted in anguish.

'And then they said that if he had not agreed to your terms, you would have raised the four provinces of Erin to carry it off!' He paused again.

'The fools were overheard,' he said. 'The thing was reported to Daire. And next morning when I went to claim the Don, he refused to loan him. I did my best to smooth over their talk. I pleaded it was merely drunken boasting. I said it was of no account and I urged your offerings again, but it was no use.'

I knew that Mac Roth was angry and bitter. It hurt his pride to have his mission undermined by drunken servants. I felt for him, but I also knew – perhaps I had always known, how it would be. For this quarrel was not about the Don Cuailnge. It was something that had been waiting a long time to happen. The bull was simply the excuse, the tinder.

I spoke decisively. 'We need not trouble with the 'whys' and 'wherefores',' I said. 'It was well known that Queen Medbh would rise against Ulster and take by force what has not been given freely.'

I waited until I saw comprehension flood into his face. Then I rose, gathered my long gown about me and headed for my private chambers.

II

WITHIN DAYS I had put the war into action. Messengers were sent at my command to the other provinces of Erin – Leinster, Munster, and also to Tara itself, the King's seat. We also alerted the Ulster exiles – all those who had left Emain after the killing of the Sons of Usna and come to me for protection. The Exiles all lived in Connacht now, banded together under Conchobar's son, Cormac Connlonges, who had stood against his father in the bloodbath sixteen years ago. Since then, for sixteen long years, the Exiles had been harrying the Ulster people, waiting for me to summon all of Erin to rise against the tyrant and defend their cause.

Fergus, of course, was with them, too. Fergus, the true king of Ulster, tricked and deposed, and now a favoured guest in my province. Fergus, who was betrayed by Conchobor first into giving up his throne, and then again when he was sent to protect the Sons of Usna. Twice duped – and he the chief warrior of the Red Branch Army. From my point of view, such a warrior was a great catch, and even my husband Ailill knew that.

As I had anticipated, the Exiles needed little summoning. Soon enough I saw them arrive, all three thousand of them, gathering on the plain of Cruachan Ai. They came in three companies. Watching as they processed in splendour, it seemed to me they had robed themselves for the three famous houses at the court of Emain Macha. The first troop was attired for the Speckled House. They were dressed in speckled cloaks, had short-cropped hair and knee-length tunics. They carried stabbing-spears and full-length shields covering their entire bodies.

The second company represented the Red Branch House. They had long red tunics reaching to the calf and dark-grey cloaks. Their hair was long and tied back on their heads. They carried smaller shields and five-barred spears. I watched intently as the two companies assembled. All the time I was looking for Cormac, Conchobor's son. Then suddenly I saw him. He was heading the third company. These surely represented the Royal Palace itself, for they entirely outstripped the other two. They wore full-length cloaks of royal purple beneath which were richly embroidered crimson tunics flowing down to their ankles. Their hair was shoulder-length, untied and blowing free. Across one arm they supported their shields, curved and scallop-edged, flashing brightly in the sun. In the other they held long delicate spears, each spear the length of a pillar from the Royal Hall.

Thus came the Ulster Exiles in their proud attire. And not long after came the troops from the other provinces of Erin. Soon all four provinces were assembled on my plain. The sight was magnificent indeed, a vast sea of armed men shining in my field, each troop being drilled by its commander. I looked at this array of nobility and splendour and thought how easily we would take Ulster with such companies.

I knew it was our right to take Ulster, and I planned to take it effortlessly. This was no idle boast. I knew I could do this because the wily Conchobor – the Usurper King, was cursed, along with all his warriors. They had been cursed by Macha, a woman of the *sidhe*. It was because Conchobor had forced her to run against his horses in her hour of childbirth. And now he and all his warriors were struck each year by violent birth pangs rendering them unfit to go to war. And now the time of their pangs was almost on them. I knew this because I had already sent out spies to Ulster.

Nevertheless, in spite of all our preparations, we were prevented from leaving. This was because, as was the custom, each company had brought their druids. And, of course, as soon as they all arrived, the druids went off together to consult the omens. It was already late in the year and I was growing impatient. But, even so, the druids held back the gathered armies on the plain waiting for the propitious signs. It was an anxious time, for the army was getting restless. Then, at last, after two long weeks, the druids said we could go. I remember ascending my tower, flooded with relief, and looking out on the great host one last time before I led them out. They were my army, all of them – my men, my splendid troops, my shining warriors. Fifty thousand hearts riding high for battle!

I gave them time to form themselves into ranks and prepare to begin the march. Then I processed out from the palace, my crescent crown shining above my yellow hair, my gorgeous robes more glorious even than those of the son of Conchobor. A great roar of cheering met me as I ascended my chariot.

'Even so, each one who leaves behind a dear friend or lover will also be cursing me now,' I murmured to my charioteer.

All he said in answer was:

'Wait, before you give the signal, wait for me to turn the chariot in the sun's path, so that I may draw down the power of blessing for our return.'

And so the chariot clattered round in a tight circle while he pulled at the bridle bits in the mouths of the eager horses. But, just as we straightened and he raised the whip, suddenly a woman appeared in front of us barring our way. It seemed as if she had come out of the air. Her hair was plaited and yellow as the sun's ball, a speckled cloak draped her shoulders, a red hood fell down her back and a long fair plait hung over it.

'Who are you?' I called out.

'Fedelm,' she answered 'a woman poet.'

'Where are you from?'

'I have come from studying poetry and the seer's art in Alba.'

'Have you the gift of *imbas forosnai?* I asked her.

'I have,' she replied.

'Then tell me with your seer's vision what is to be the fate of my army?'

In answer the woman went into trance while all the troops and horses waited.

'Seer!' I asked, 'Fedelm, what do you see?'

Her eyes showed their whites like those of a horse in flight.

'I see blood-red, I see crimson!' she answered.

All the troops could hear her trance-like voice, for her words were carried on the wind across the plain.

'That cannot be!' I retorted, sending my voice bellowing after hers for all to hear. 'Conchobor and all the men of Ulster are overcome with the Pangs of Macha. I have had word. Look again!'

But still she showed only the whiteness and her flickering eyelids:

'I see blood-red, and I see crimson!'

'No, Prophetess!' I shouted hotly. 'Conchobor's son Cuscraid Mend, 'the Stammerer' is also in his pains, as is his other son Celtchar, and a third of Ulster's warriors with him. I have had word of this too. Look again!'

'I see blood-red, I see crimson.'

'But Eogan Durthacht's son is also in his pains, and we have Fergus and the Ulster Exiles on our side. What have we to fear from Ulster!'

Again she intoned:

'I see blood-red, I see crimson!'

Her words were beginning to threaten the morale of the troops. I raised my voice.

'That,' I said decisively, 'is but the colour of war, the colour of wrath, of battle wounds. It is appropriate to our mission, nothing more. So, tell me, Fedelm, what, beyond the war-colour do you see?'

> 'I see a man in battle, yellow-haired
> girdled at the waist with blood,
> around his head the sun's full halo.
> Victory is on his brow.
> The iris of his eye reflects
> the seven jewels of the hero.
> His jaw is a fearful battle snarl.
> Yet he is fair and draws the love of women.

> It is a giant – yet one man, I see.
> One man against the host of Erin.
> But I see the troops against him drowned
> in crimson by his hand alone;
> It is Cuchulainn, the Hound of Ulster.'

'One man,' I thought. 'Cuchulainn. I did not know this man. It was the first time I had heard his name.'

I looked at my troops spread out on the green, all eighteen cantrevs of them, restless and eager to set out. How could we fail? And so, with Fedelm still screeching out her warning I gave my signal.

I raised my royal staff, and rode out before the host of thousands. I lead them out while all the troops were ripe for action. We had to be swift because it was the closing of the year. We left on the Monday after the feast of Samhain. Behind me came all the host of Erin united against the Ulster tyrant and his warriors, who were even now helpless in their labour pangs. It seemed impossible that we would not succeed. I expected swift victory. I planned to return before the Solstice fires of winter. After all there was only Cuchulainn, one man – apparently untouched by Macha's curse, to come against us.

III

WE MADE our first camp at Cuil Silinne. Ailill's tent was set up beside my own, his bedding and coverings spread out and arranged for him by our servants. On the far side of Ailill's was Fergus' tent, and beyond his that of Cormac Conlongas, the king's son. Beyond him again, was Fiacha, grandson of Conchobor. Thus were the men ranged in rank and order. On the other side of me lay my daughter Findabhar of the fair-brow.

While the servants were still setting out our things, I called for my ring of chariots. Horses were harnessed, first to my own chariot and then to the other eight that were grouped in pairs around me to keep the dust and sods from splattering my robes and crown. I had my hair braided and put up, I wore my tunic of royal sammet against my white skin, I had my purple cloak draped over me and the heavy crown of Cruachan set on my head. Thus I went out to inspect the troops, with black lines of khol round my eyes and berry juice to stain my lips. Not for nothing do they call me queen, for in all of Erin, I am the last woman to rule over any province. And not for nothing have I been called 'The Intoxicating One'.

As I made my circuit, I felt the force of my intoxication, I felt the mantle of my regal power, my beauty, my stateliness and my perfection settle on the men. Every man I passed turned to look at me. I saw the awe on his face and I took his worship. Some think that is a heavy burden. Only when women have forgotten how to rule, forgotten that it is their birthright, would that be so. Yet, while I shed my woman's power upon the men, I kept a man's head on me. Eighteen troops I had, three thousand men apiece, but as I made my circuit, one troop, I saw clearly, threatened to outshine them all. For, among all the others, I noticed that the men of Leinster were first to pitch camp and roof their dwelling, the first to cook their feast and afterwards to recline and hear their harpers. Their skills were impressive. Too impressive.

When I returned, I was deep in thought. I said to Ailill:

'There is one troop that will bring trouble on this venture.'

'Which troop?' he asked.

'The men of Leinster.'

'Why, what is wrong with them?'

'Nothing. On the contrary, they outshine the others in their speed, their training and their eagerness.'

'Then what is the problem?'

'When the war is finished, they will take all the credit.'

I was thinking of my own standing, and also of potential strife between the armies.

'But they are fighting for us?' Ailill objected.

It was pitiful that he could see no further than that.

'It would be better if they did not come with us.' I said.

I saw the exasperation on his face, his ready anger. Then he saw my fixed look and shrugged.

'All right then, let them stay,' he said.

'That would be the most foolish course to take!'

'What do you mean?'

'If we leave them behind,' I said acidly, 'they will attack us from the rear and take our land.'

I was wondering how the man could be so stupid.

Findabhar said quietly:

'What is to be done then, if they can neither come with us nor be left behind?'

I gave the most pitiless answer. It was the way a strategist might end the matter.

'We shall have to kill them,' I said. My voice was expressionless.

'Now I know it is a woman speaking!' retorted Ailill, 'they must be killed just because they pitch their tents too quickly!'

I drew in my breath, preparing to say my piece. But then Fergus, who had kept quiet until now, spoke up sharply.

'The men of Leinster are the allies of the Ulster Exiles. We have a treaty with them. If they are to be killed you will have to kill them over the dead bodies of the Ulster Exiles!'

It was no more than I had expected. Nevertheless I had to show him who was in command.

'Even if your Ulster Exiles stood against us, we would hardly be outnumbered!' I said scornfully. 'As well as my own two troops, there are my seven sons, the Maines, each with a troop apiece. That's nine to two, counting your one troop together with the troop of Leinster!'

'You miscount!' cried Fergus, eyeing me as if in combat. 'The seven kings of Munster, each with a cantrev apiece would come forward for us, as well as my own and the troop of Leinster. Thus could I do battle with you, even in the middle of this host of armies – nine to nine!'

I met his look. The field on which we played was equal. His wit was sharp. At times like this, I knew his worth. I knew him for the true king of Ulster. But, as soon as we had tried and matched our powers, he said:

'Nevertheless, I will not insist on combat over this matter, for the solution is simple. In order to prevent the warriors of Leinster lording it over the rest of the army, I propose we break up their troop and redistribute them among the others. We have seventeen troops, in all. Theirs is the eighteenth and can be spread around. That way they will reinforce our army and no longer threaten it.'

His plan was excellent. How we might work together, he and I! But I would not show him how impressed I was.

'I do not care what happens to them,' I said dismissively, 'as long as their troop is broken up.'

Fergus went out then and by next morning the warriors were already split up and spread among the other troops, like leavening yeast. Even so, next day the men of Leinster showed their superior prowess. We set out for Moin Coltna, the moor near Cottain. On the way a huge herd of deer came into our path and some of the Leinster warriors were the first to catch and kill them. It was just as well they were scattered among the troops or we would have had rivalry and trouble even before encountering our enemy. This was the time for bonding, the time for sharing strength, as well I knew.

Nevertheless, I soon discovered it was not only strife among the troops I had to watch for.

Later that day we reached the Plain of Trego. The early evening gloom forced us to halt there. The men struck camp and that night we were assailed by some kind of evil shadow. The pall of Nemain, the spirit of fear, seemed to come over the entire army. In the darkness of the night Dubtech, the Ulster warrior, called by the men 'the black one', spoke a prophetic warning, which soon began to spread panic among the ranks.

'You march into dark,' he chanted in his sing-song voice,
'for the man will come, one man –
a match against a host

to guard his kingdom.
Even the river Cronn will rise to help him
barring the warrior's way.
In the final combat, one third only of the host
will be left with Medbh, the flesh of countless warriors
flung far by the One in battle frenzy … '

As soon as I heard his wailing words, I came up to him and stopped his chanting. My eyes were blazing with anger as I ordered him to stop indulging in such foreboding. Then I went among the men. It took time but I outfaced the prophecies with a mixture of scorn and reassurance. It was my power, a woman's power, but at last I calmed them.

Next morning we formed our ranks and prepared to march again. It was no easy thing to keep such a number in order, for each army was led by its own king, each troop by its chief, and smaller bands had captains over them. Up to a point this worked quite well, but there was the ever-present threat of internal feuding. We also needed to keep the task ahead of us clearly in sight. For this, I decided, we needed someone to go ahead and find out what moves, if any, the enemy were making. We took counsel as to who we should appoint for the task and Fergus seemed the obvious choice, for he knew Ulster and the likely movements of the Red Branch warriors. Moreover for him the war was obligatory, for he was coming against his own usurper.

So we sent Fergus ahead and he, in turn, sent messengers to scout for news of Ulster's army. Acting on the information he received, he advised us to turn south, whereupon the whole army wheeled round and took a different course. But now the terrain was difficult and after a few days I began to feel we were making little progress.

Fergus was well out in front of the troops when I rode ahead and caught up with him.

'Something is not right,' I said. 'What road is this we're on? It feels like a detour, for we're crossing all kinds of rough land. Even Ailill is beginning to suspect some kind of treachery on your part. Or is it just that you are uncertain of the path? If your old allegiance to Ulster is making you do this, it would be better to appoint another in your place.'

My words burned in the air, my meaning was unmistakeable. Fergus answered hotly:

'What is the matter with you, Medbh! Of course I am not being disloyal, I'm merely taking us on a roundabout route in order to avoid Cuchulainn. But if you doubt me I shall go to the rear of the army and you can put someone else in my place!'

I said nothing, but he knew now that I was suspicious. He had answered me cleverly, for at that time I was unaware that he'd already sent messengers to warn the men of Ulster of our coming. Thus the route, as I half-suspected, was his way of delaying our approach until the Pangs of Macha left the Ulster warriors.

Even so, after my warning, Fergus took a straighter route and soon we came towards Iraird Cuillen. Riding ahead of us were the two warriors Err and Innal with their charioteers. They were bearing our precious things, our rugs and cloaks and jewels to keep them from being spoiled by the dust clouds created by our army. When we saw they had stopped ahead of us, we slowed down, and gradually the whole host came to a halt.

Fergus reached them first. They had halted beside a strange sign. It was a sapling oak bent into a hoop and fixed onto a pillar stone.

'What has happened?' I shouted as I rode up quickly. 'Why have we stopped?'

'We have stopped because of this spancel-hoop,' said Fergus. 'There is a message cut in *ogham* on it.'

'What does it say?'

The hoop was carried over to him and he took some time deciphering the lines.

'Let no man pass until one is found to forge a hoop like this – one-handed from a single branch,' he read, 'except for my master

Fergus.' He looked up and caught my eye.

'It is the work of Cuchulainn,' he said.

Then he gave the hoop to the druids.

'Tell us the riddle of the hoop,' he said, 'who put it there and why?'

The druids looked at the *ogham* symbols and discussed among themselves. Then one came forward:

'It was made by one hand', he said, 'and by a champion. It is intended as a trap, a barrier to stop the progress of the army. It should not be dismissed unless one of you can match the deed.'

Fergus took me aside.

'If you overlook this omen,' he said, 'you will rouse such fury in the man that cut it that he will descend on us in the night and we'll find a whole host killed by morning.'

Ailill came up:

'We've no need to invite any killings so early on,' he said, 'Let's turn south. We can pass into Ulster through the neck of the forest at Fid Duin instead of by this crossing.'

Deciding I had no need of a further night's panic among my troops, I agreed. So we turned south and cut our way through the thinnest part of the forest, slashing through trunks and branches to hew out a path for our chariots.

The moment we crossed into Ulster, the temperature dropped and it seemed to become unnaturally cold. We decided to strike camp, but the fires we lit were throttled by a squall of heavy snow. Soon the chariots were buried to their wheel-tips and men were wading through it waist-deep. It was impossible to pitch tents, raise booths, rest or sleep. The air was so dense with snow, it blotted out the sight of one man from another. We had a terrible night, being neither able to sleep, eat, or go forward. At the first weak light of dawn, we began digging tracks for the chariots and our efforts were rewarded, for the sun came up like a bright blessing and the snow miraculously shrank beneath us as we pushed on further into Ulster. As before, Err and Innel rode ahead in their chariots.

We made good progress that day, and the sun still held the sky when we approached the ford of Ath Gabla. Then, suddenly we heard a commotion ahead and a terrible sight met our eyes. The headless bodies of Err and Innel and their charioteers were rushing towards us, the chariots awash with blood and their horses mad-eyed and screeching with fear. We suspected an ambush, but when we came up to the ford we saw only a forked tree standing upright in the water. On its pronged branches were four heads swaying above the river.

We look around cautiously. But there were no Ulster warriors waiting to ambush us, nothing but the dripping heads of our men and the tree fork. On one side of the fork we saw a message cut in *ogham*. The message said:

'One man has thrown this fork with one hand, nor shall any pass until a man among you throws it one-handed – excepting Fergus.'

'It seems astonishing to me how quickly the men were struck!' said Ailill.

'That is not what is astonishing,' replied Fergus, drily. 'The striking of the forked branch from the trunk in one blow and the thrusting of it in the river with the throw of one hand – that is what is astonishing!'

I looked hard into Fergus' eyes.

'Undo this for us!' I said.

It was a command.

He met my gaze.

'Very well,' he said.

My command was necessary, not only in order to outface the *geis* that had been put on us, but with the forked tree blocking the ford, the company was brought to a complete halt, for none of our chariots could get past.

'I'll pull it out', said Fergus, 'and see if it was indeed cut with one blow!'

A chariot was brought, one of the simpler ones. Fergus mounted it and yoked it to the forked tree. But as soon as he began to pull, the whole thing cracked beneath him, the floor broke and the wheels fell away. Soon it was nothing but a pile of jagged splinters.

Fergus called for another chariot to be brought, and then another. When he had reduced seventeen chariots to heaps of wood and metal, I cried out:

'Stop! That is enough! You are not to ruin any more of our chariots!'

'Besides,' I added 'this effort has caused so much delay that if we'd been able to get through, by now we would have ventured far into Ulster and be heading home with our plunder.'

I glared at Fergus. I suspected he was again deliberately delaying us.

Fergus caught my look. He set his jaw and called for one last chariot, a swift one. I ordered it myself and made sure it was his own chariot that was brought.

As I had thought, it took Fergus only one tug with his own chariot to raise the forked tree and, this time, there was not a single creak from the floor, spindle, or wheelhousing. Fergus lifted the tree out in one smooth movement and gave it to Ailill.

Ailill examined it.

'It was indeed cut with a single stroke,' he said, 'a single stroke from root to top. We need to know more about this man.'

By now the light in the sky was already thickening and the men were chilled and hungry from the previous night. Ailill ordered that camp be struck. Booths and tents were erected and, at my command, in order to raise the morale, special feasts were prepared, with harpers for entertainment.

After we had eaten I sat with Ailill and Fergus. Ailill looked across at Fergus.

'What sort of man is this Hound of Ulster?' he asked.

As Fergus considered his reply I cut in:

'Is he the hardest man to deal with in Ulster?'

Fergus looked away and a soft light came into his eyes.

'He is my foster-son', he said, 'so I know him well. There is no fiercer hero, no man able to perform such feats as he, no warrior who can outdo him in courage, agility or prowess.'

It seemed to me this claim was outrageous. It was clearly the fond assessment of a foster father. After a silence, Ailill asked quietly:

'How old is he?'

Fergus laughed.

'I can soon tell you that,' he said, 'but his age is not the issue. He joined the boy troop when he was only five. Since that time he has trained with Scathach the warrior woman in Alba.'

He paused.

'Well?' asked Ailill.

'He is seventeen years old.'

When I heard that I laughed out loud.

'Why, he is no god!' I retorted, 'he bleeds from his wounds like any other man. So far he has not even shown himself – no doubt for fear of being captured!'

I turned with a triumphant gaze and caught Ailill's eye.

'Why on earth should we fear this beardless youth, this young elf who is no older than an adolescent girl waiting for marriage! Besides he is still untried!'

I laughed again, but Fergus shook his head and stared out through the opening of our booth.

'That is not so,' he said, 'for he has already accomplished extraordinary feats, in spite of his young age.'

We sat up late that night, listening to Fergus relating Cuchulainn's deeds of prowess, until I tired of such stories and retired to my tent.

IV

THE NEXT day we made our way to Mag Muceda, the Pig-keeper's Plain. Here we were brought to a halt yet again by another mysterious barrier, apparently also the work of this young upstart warrior. This time he had cut down an oak tree and laid it across the path with an *ogham* message cut into its side. His message demanded that no one was to pass the oak until one of the warriors had managed to leap successfully across it in his chariot on a first attempt.

Because of this the rest of the day was a mess. Hundreds of warriors tried to do the feat and all failed. Thirty more chariots ended up a smashed heap of splinters, several horses were lamed, and we were obliged to stay the night there without further progress.

Next morning, an eager host were again raring to try the feat, but I refused to put any more chariots and horses at risk. Instead I put another plan into force. I sent for Fraech mac Fidaig, a man among my army who was also the leader of the *sidhe* – a man so fair that all women loved him. Fraech himself loved Findabhar, my daughter. Nevertheless, Ailill and I had kept them from marrying because we feared the jealousy of other kings. After this war, perhaps we could think again.

Fraech was found among the troops and appeared before me. His perfect, white-limbed body, the easy way he moved, his grey eyes, his lean cheekbones and noble brow, made every woman turn her head.

I turned a beseeching gaze on him.

'Help us, Fraech,' I implored him. 'Rid us of this constraint. Go and fight Cuchulainn for us.'

Next morning, Fraech went out just after dawn with a company of nine men. As I watched them go, a ray of rose-coloured sun touched Fraech's silvery hair.

I was restless all day, waiting for news. When at last I heard the horsemen returning. Fraech was not among them. One of the riders came on ahead. He was panting, his face pale.

'What happened?' I asked him.

'My Lady, we rode to the ford of Ath Fuait, and saw Cuchulainn bathing in the river. He looked no more than a child. His flesh was almost as white as that of Fraech, his face beardless, except for a few strands of yellow hair. We pulled up. We felt we could not simply plunge into the river and butcher him. Fraech told us to wait while he stripped off. He went to the water's edge and Cuchulainn called out:

'Don't come any nearer or I shall kill you!'

'Certainly I shall come,' replied Fraech. 'But I will meet you in the water and play fair with you.'

''Whatever you say,' said Cuchulainn.

Then Fraech suggested one-handed combat with each man's hand wrapped around the other. Cuchulainn agreed and so Fraech met him in the water.

A long time they wrestled together but then Cuchulainn pushed Fraech underneath the water and kept him there. After a while he raised him. Fraech was almost drowned, but as his heaving lungs drank the air and spat out water, Cuchulainn shouted:

'Now will you yield to me?'

'Never!' replied Fraech as soon as he could speak.

So Cuchulainn thrust him once more down under the water. He never came up alive.'

A deadly silence came over the men who heard the tale. I remembered how that morning, a bloody dawn had touched Fraech, and, for a moment, I fancied we were labouring under a curse. But I shook my mind free and commanded that the formalities be attended to. At my bidding Fraech's body was carried back from the ford and laid out in ceremony. The whole company filed past to mourn him. Men as well as women were weeping.

Late in the evening, a strange mist rose from the land, and a company of women appeared. They were wearing green tunics and moved together in a slow procession with bowed heads. They were the women of the *sidhe* come to bear their king away. They lifted him between them and carried him into their mound. Deep into the night we heard the aching mournful music of their lamenting.

At first light, Fergus called for his chariot, harnessed the horses, and, as I had wished from the beginning, made a run at the oak. His chariot sprang over it, horses and all. Then the men dragged the tree away and we set off.

But Cuchulainn was lying in wait and, as we marched, he crept up on us and, armed only with a sling, picked off six of my warriors. One of my hounds ran ahead and Cuchulainn aimed a stone at its head. We caught up with its headless corpse flailing in a pool of blood.

I stopped my chariot and bent over the young dog. Then I turned towards the troops.

'We are mocked!' I cried. 'What is the matter with you? How much longer will you let this trickster prey on us?'

After I had taunted them, the men whipped their horses into frenzy. They took off after Cuchulainn, some driving their chariots so fast over the rough ground that they broke their chariot shafts. But he evaded all their efforts.

We went over a high place, and when we descended again and came into woodland I sent the charioteers out to chop down branches to make new chariot poles. Unknown to them, Cuchulainn was hiding amongst the trees. The next thing we knew, a charioteer came running towards us, the wind of fear on his face. There was something dangling at his back that rocked as he ran and sprayed blood to either side of him. When he reached us, he fetched the thing from his back. It was the head of our son, Orlam.

'Cuchulainn overcame him in combat,' panted the charioteer. 'And he ordered me to run with it on my back to you, like this!'

He had barely finished speaking when a stone hit the back of his head and smashed it in front of us. Blood and pieces of flesh were on my robes, while the head of my son went rolling across the grass.

'This is hardly killing birds!' I said. I was emotionless.

As we retreated into the camp, I thought of the youthful boy and the damage he was doing. If he wanted to taunt us he was doing well. I had many sons among my company, but each was precious. There would be time for keening after the war was ended. Instead I went white with fury. Three of my warriors armed themselves and their charioteers and went to the ford of Garach, seeking to ambush Cuchulainn. It was six men against one, breaking the rules of combat, but royal blood had now been spilled, and we sought swift revenge. When their chariots returned with six lifeless bodies slopping in their own blood, there was growing disbelief and anger as well as keening in the camp that night.

It seemed as if Cuchulainn had heard my remark about birds, for, next day, before we had time to break camp, a great stone hurtled towards Ailill, knocking the pet bird that he carried on his shoulder to the ground. Before I had time to react, a second stone flew past my ear and took the squirrel from my own shoulder. As we scrambled inside our booth, I thought I could hear derisory laughter coming from somewhere among the branches.

Ailill was looking at me, wide-eyed with shock. It was the nearness of our own deaths we were feeling.

'He cannot be far away!' said Ailill. All seven Maines, our sons, were with us and they immediately stretched their heads over the bothy fence to see if they could spot him. Not a branch moved, nor a leaf shook. They were bringing their heads down again when there was a thud and one of them fell dead, hit by a flying stone.

'That was a clever way to rise up against him,' retorted Maenen the jester. 'And after all your boasting, too. I'm sure *I* could have knocked his head off!'

But even as he spoke, his own head joined the other, his brains splattered by another great stone.

'I swear by the gods themselves,' shouted Ailill, 'I'll slice any man in two who dares to mock Cuchulainn after this!'

It was almost impossible to track Cuchulainn while he prowled around the forest and preyed on us in this way. At last Ailill said:

'Let's break camp and keep moving, day and night if necessary until we reach Cuailnge. If we wait around any more, this man will single-handedly kill two thirds of our army.'

As he spoke, strange musical strains rose around the camp. It was the sound of harps but not as our harpers played, it was more like the enchanted music of the *sidhe*. It was the sleep strain they were playing, magical music to allay our grief and to heal the hearts of the warriors. I would gladly have succumbed to such sounds, for two sons of mine were already taken and my heart was in need of curing. Besides, I did not think the company of harpers were of evil intent, for it was well known Fraech of the *sidhe* had been fighting for us.

But such was the horror on my armies and fear of omens, that without my command, a band of warriors gave chase to the harpers. As soon as they knew they were pursued, the sweet-voiced company shape-changed into deer and ran, fleet-footed, to the stones of Liac Mor where the warriors ceased pursuing them. I knew then that they were not the *sidhe*, but powerful shamen of the druids. Yet I still think they only meant to mend us.

Not long afterwards our army broke camp again and we marched forward. The warrior Lethan 'the Broad' rode ahead with a great anger burning within him and lay in wait at the next ford to ambush Cuchulainn. But when our hosts came up to the ford, we found his head lying beside his body, and that of his charioteer flung onto the shoulder of the hill beyond.

The morale of the men was dwindling and I knew we needed to take action. If there was no army for us to meet, then we could at least make our mark on the land. I held a parley, and several of the kings of Erin, incensed at the situation, called for us to begin ravaging the land. First they wanted to burn Mag Breg, then Meath, then the plain of Conall and after that the plain of Muirthemne. As the plan was being discussed, I looked at Fergus' face. When Muirthemne was mentioned, I saw him flinch, for this was Cuchulainn's home territory. But he quickly composed his face, trying to hide his reaction from me.

Following Ailill's decision, we kept marching until we reached the province of Cuailnge. We laid the country waste as we went, burning the woodland, the crops, and even the cropped grasses of the plains. There were no Ulstermen to withstand us, as they were still in pangs and rendered weaker than their women. Strangely, in all that time, Cuchulainn left us alone.

As soon as we entered Cuailnge we made camp and it was here that my serving woman, Lochu went down to the river to fetch water for me. She was wearing one of my gold coronets, but two stones from Cuchulainn's sling struck her on the head. We found her with her head crushed and the coronet broken in pieces. Now the boy had stooped low, indeed! Was it my own head that he thought to crush? Or was he merely being indiscriminate in his pickings in order to spread fear among the army? After this the men were afraid even to go outside to relieve themselves. As for myself, whenever I went out, I commanded a company of men to form a hedge of shields around me.

V

WHEN WE reached the place called Finnabair in the province of Cuailnge, I saw that the only way ahead involved going over a mountain. The pass was narrow and it would take a long time for the troops and all our cattle to get through. It was then that a good plan came to me.

'Let us divide the army,' I said, 'Let half go with Ailill and take the road by Midluachair, and let the other half go with Fergus and myself by the pass of Bernas Bo Ulad.'

Fergus protested:

'That means we have the difficult half. We will never get the cattle across the mountain without cutting a gap in it.'

'Then let a gap be cut,' I said.

I wanted the land to feel my power upon it. I wanted Ulster, after this, to be changed forever. I also wanted time with Fergus.

I was not unaware of the torn loyalties the former Red Branch chief was experiencing. Cuchulainn was his foster son, the object of his pride. He might have quarrelled with King Conchobor, but never with Cuchulainn himself, even though he was now the king's own champion. I already suspected Fergus of causing delays, of sending messages to Cuchulainn. This I could understand. But we also needed the deposed King of Ulster to stay on our side, and it seemed to me he needed just a little more persuasion.

After Ailill had left with his half of the troops, I sent our troops on ahead and called Fergus to me. The look I gave him could hardly be mistaken. My lips were moist, my colour high, my breath was coming in shallow bursts.

'I think we need a private talk,' I said.

I drew him away towards the woods at Cluithre. I had noticed the way he had been looking at me night after night. I had heard of his prodigious appetite. His capacious lust was legendary, as was his sexual prowess. Not for the first time did I feel the two of us would be well matched.

I wetted my lips again. Slowly this time, letting my red tongue stroke round them. My eyes were large and dark. My hair was blown in fluted tendrils round my neck, my robe had eased its way across one shoulder, baring my arm beneath a thin, silk tunic. The day was spring-like. The gods were on my side.

I stood with my back against the warm bole of a tree. I ran my fingers up and down a branch of it. The look I gave Fergus was half way between a queen's command and a young maid's passion. He brought his jaw down hard on me and worked his lips against mine. Slowly I yielded to him. First he had my lips, and then my bared shoulders. After that I let him plunge his hand inside my robe and feel my breasts, my thighs, my readiness …

A long time we lay there. Much was our inventiveness and many were the times we satisfied each other. A queen and a king. It had been a long wait.

At last Fergus got up and pulled on his robes. Then he began looking about for his sword.

'This is terrible!' he said suddenly.

'Why, what is the matter?' I asked.

'I have done wrong to Ailill,' he said. In a fluster, he added:

'Wait here while I go into the wood. But I may be gone for a while.'

I was puzzled.

What I learned later was that his sword had been stolen from its scabbard while we lay together. Not only that, it was taken by one of Ailill's men. If I'd known then that Ailill had sent someone to spy on us I would have been very angry. For Ailill knew only too well that my sexual favours were not just for him, they were also to be used for the good of our cause.

A short time later, Fergus returned with what looked like a sword stuck into his scabbard. He had been fashioning a substitute out of wood, but as yet I did not know this. He must have thought the stealing of his sword too shameful a thing to divulge.

'Let us hurry and catch up our troops,' he said.

We went through the mountain pass with all our troops and cattle and met up with the other wing of the army who were already camped on the plain beyond. As we were setting up our own camp, Ailill invited Fergus to play a game of *fidchell* with him.

I was sitting in the booth beside Ailill when Fergus entered. Ailill glanced up as he came in and began to laugh quietly. I raised an enquiring eyebrow at Fergus. He sat down heavily and looked meaningfully at Ailill.

'It is better to be laughed at than to be made mad by the act,' Fergus said carefully.

When there was no response he added:

'The tip of my sword was also maddened.'

Then he began claiming he had come against the armies of Ulster in a wild rage. But Ailill knew he had not fought with the enemy for he had no sword with which to carry out his boasted prowess.

He looked levelly at Fergus.

'Why do you rage so much?' he asked. 'It seems to me you have done well enough without your weapon. I hear you've managed to scale the heights of a royal belly, and worked your way into a royal ford. Your so-called heroism is nothing but an empty swagger.'

Ailill looked in triumph at Fergus' discomfort. Then he said magnanimously:

'Now sit down and play *fidchell* with me.'

Ailill began setting out the pieces of the Royal Game on the bronze board. Gold for himself and silver for Fergus. As he handed the silver king to Fergus he said:

'The kings and queens are rulers of the game, surrounded by their keen armies.'

He set down his own gold queen and glanced at Fergus.

'I am well acquainted with women and queens', he said.

When Fergus made no reply, he added, as if musing aloud:

'The fault lies with them, for it is the power of their sweet mounds and swellings that causes the noblest of men to raise his thrusting sword.'

Then he opened the game and they began to play, each with careful strategy stalking each other's king.

'It is not right,' observed Ailill when they had been playing for a while, 'that a dear little king on the gilded point should face death on this crazy board.'

He looked at his gold queen.

'Ah, great Medbh,' he said, 'not quite so secure now. I think I shall advance these druids against Fergus after all. Right should win out, don't you think, even in a game?' He looked up challengingly at Fergus.

'Stop this fooling!' I said sharply. I was worried about the leaders grouped around us who were following the game. 'Don't forget,' I said, 'we have no idea what lies in store for us. There's Ulster's Boy Troop for one. Everything could change at any moment and, in any case,' I added, looking meaningfully at Ailill, 'if a man is wise he should be able to rise above petty grudges. Don't be like the enemy holding onto their cattle against all odds!'

When Ailill said nothing, Fergus added:

'Yes, my friend, it's a shame to bandy words with each other in front of our men. Just think where it could all end! For you know as well as I do that if fair words turn foul, then right becomes wrong, and the next thing we know there will be kings at each other's throats and bloody blades to wipe - all because of a harsh word spoken out of turn!'

They abandoned their game then. But I lay awake that night thinking again of how well we might work together, Fergus and I. Between us we had placated Ailill and avoided a dangerous scene in front of our army's leaders. Fergus was a conciliator it seemed, as well as a strategist. But most of all, it was as a lover that I thought of him. It was not the first time I had dwelt on the memory of our time together in the woods of Cluithre.

Next morning Ailill made a speech that alarmed me. It sounded like a prophecy:

'There is one man who stands against great armies,' he said, 'and now the waters of the Cronn are unleashed like his great deeds upon the Connacht warriors. Soon there will be tides of blood flowing from cut necks, deaths of our greatest chiefs and waves rising where the beardless boy lies waiting.'

'Stop, Ailill, great son of Mata!' I shouted. 'Don't summon any more death and violence. Remember our chariot raids, all the women and cattle we have captured and the swords we have broken!'

'And don't forget,' cried Fergus: 'all the heads that are stuck on the front of our chariots. All lion-hearted warriors caught up in a quarrel over queens.'

I did not understand his meaning. It seemed he was speaking in riddles. But I sensed his mood had changed. It was harsher, more bellicose. I said quickly:

'Whatever you may say Fergus, Ailill bows to you. The host is on the move and you have the mastery.' I paused while I let this flattery take effect. Then I added quietly:

'Now that Ailill's power is in your hands, what do you intend to do?'

I looked at the Ulster chieftain. I needed to know where he stood with our army. He returned my gaze, but the question hung unanswered in the air between us.

That day we marched on until we came to the River Cronn. One of our sons – one of the seven Maines, ran up to Ailill.

'Quickly!' he said, send me out ahead of the herds and let me come against Cuchulainn!'

Before Ailill could reply Fergus spoke for him.

'Don't go,' he said sharply, 'unless you want to lose your head at the hands of the beardless boy! For consider the power he has, and how much he has hurt your father, and made a mockery of your mother!'

He turned a steely eye on me. He seemed almost contemptuous.

'Let me take the Exiles and go on ahead,' he said, 'so that I can ensure the boy receives fair play. We'll drive the cattle in front of us and keep the armies behind us and the women at the rear.'

I was outraged. After all I had given him, he was trying to help Cuchulainn again! Cuchulainn who had harried the armies of the whole of Erin and made a fool of me! But even in the heat of the moment I kept a cool head. I knew I needed Fergus on my side, but I also needed to hold my authority. I spoke up haughtily and loud enough for all the leaders of the troops to hear.

'Give me your oath, Fergus, that you will guard our cattle, and that your army will hold off the Ulstermen. Otherwise, ' I paused and looked at him. I was shaking with anger but I kept my voice clear and steady: 'Otherwise I swear by the gods of my tribe that all the armies from the Plain of Ai will rise up with a roar of rage and come against you!'

Fergus turned a burning face on me:

'Have you no shame!' he cried, 'that you dare to threaten me in front of all these people? I tell you this much, it's no soft-hearted son of mine who's caught up in this battle with Emain!'

I had never seen him so furious. He seemed beside himself with rage. At last he spat out:

'I won't raise my hand against my own people any longer. So you can stop telling me what to do. Now let me out from under your yoke, for I swear I'll never again bow to you or do your bidding!'

Obviously the thing could not easily be settled between us. Fergus had insulted my son, declared himself an Ulsterman and flouted my authority. Nevertheless the Exiles were still marching with me and Fergus might yet be tamed. That day we set out with the host and progressed as far as the ford on the River Cronn. We reckoned that Cuchulainn would be waiting for us there. But as our son rode out to meet him with a company of thirty horsemen, we witnessed a strange happening. The River Cronn began to rise. In the ensuing panic and confusion, Cuchulainn slew the Maine and his thirty horsemen. All the while the river kept rising until it seemed to lick the treetops. A further thirty of our men were drowned before the flood subsided.

'Now,' I thought, as I mourned the death of yet another of my sons at the hands of the brutal boy, 'now he even commands the rivers and they answer him.' It seemed to me that the old ways were quickly changing. As I gave in to my grief, I thought of the age-old power of woman over the land. 'What had happened to her sovereignty?' I wondered, and the thought tempted me, for a moment, to despair.

Soon enough, however, I made myself put aside my grief and address the business of our war. It seemed to me that if the power of the goddess was waning, I must put on the mind of man and rely on strategy and good tactics. Cuchulainn's furtive nightly forays were causing panic among the army. I had tried belittling him, but perhaps it was time to acknowledge the status of the boy. I needed to show him respect and offer him some kind of terms. So I called for the warrior Lugaid, and sent him to parley with Cuchulainn.

The result of this seemed promising. Cuchulainn reached an agreement that he would spare Lugaid's troops and those of the Ulster exiles in return for food and the services of our healers.

When Lugaid returned he saw that Fergus was in Ailill's tent. Lugaid called him out and related the terms to him privately. As they conferred, from inside the tent Ailill burst out:

'What is all this whispering! Is it some kind of game we are playing here! How is it that amongst all our great army, Lugaid asks favours for Fergus, the one who plays king in my place, the one who climbed to this station on the thighs of Medbh! Well, I've had enough of these secret meetings! Why shouldn't my own men go into the protected tents and avoid the flying boulders!'

Hearing this, Fergus sent Lugaid out to Cuchulainn again with a roast ox and a barrel of wine and after that Ailill's personal troop was allowed to mingle with the Exiles and share their protection. In this way both Fergus and Ailill were placated and the threatened rift between the three of us was averted.

But although he spared some of the troops, Cuchulainn went on harassing the men from the other troops, and some nights he picked off as many as a hundred warriors.

'Soon you will be in a worse situation,' Fergus said grimly to me. 'When the men of Ulster rise up from their pangs, they will grind you to pieces!'

Ailill muttered: 'If this goes on, we'll end up losing our whole army!'

I decided it was time to try and win Cuchulainn to our side. I sent Fiachu to offer Cuchulainn recompense for the ruining of his land and estates, and for any Ulstermen we had killed. On top of that I told him to offer unlimited food, drink and entertainment if he would come into my service, and to tell him it would be much more fitting for him to serve me than the petty lord of Ulster.

It was a bold try and, indeed, I felt I had right on my side. For hadn't I got all of Erin with me, as well as Fergus, the king's own son – besides all the Ulster exiles? Nevertheless, Cuchulainn was outraged at my suggestion that he served a mere lordling. He asked how I dared be so scornful of the best king in all Erin and vowed he would never betray his own mother's brother.

But despite his outrage, Cuchulainn agreed to parley with Fergus and myself. And so early the next day we went out to meet him. We saw him coming towards us as we neared the Fochaine valley. I had, by now, expected him to be something of a giant, so ferocious were his deeds and such was his reputation, but I was shocked to see how slight he was. He seemed little more than a gangly youth. I said to Fergus:

'Is that the great Hound of Ulster you were telling us about? If so, it surely wouldn't take much of a warrior to hold him off from harrying our troops!'

'However young he looks,' Fergus replied, 'there is no warrior who can single-handedly resist him.'

'In that case, ' I said, 'I'll offer him terms he'd be foolish to refuse.'

When Cuchulainn came up to us I said:

'Great Hound of Ulster, already highly praised in song, we've come to ask you to stop harrying us with your sling, for the great skill you have with it has wrecked and upset our whole army.'

'Medbh, daughter of Eochan,' he replied, 'I am no low-ranking soldier. While I have breath in my body I swear I will never stop troubling the army who are raiding Cuailnge.'

'If,' I answered, 'you will agree to stop using your sling, brave warrior, I will return to Ulster half the cows and half the women that we have taken on our raids.'

Cuchulainn bit back at me: 'I tell you I will agree to nothing unless you return every animal and every woman, free or slave, that you have taken!'

'You ask too much!' I said between my teeth. After slaughtering so many of our troops, you cannot expect us to relinquish all our spoils and be left with only the horses and tackle – and all for the sake of one man!'

'Then I will no longer bandy words with you, for I am more skilled with deeds than words!' said Cuchulainn. And with that he turned and began walking off.

'Are you not aware, O highborn son of Dechtire' I shouted after him, 'how valuable the terms are that we are offering! Do you not know that they are the most generous ever made. How dare you say they are not good enough!'

I returned to the camp burning with anger. But that night we lost another hundred men. The morale of the troops was lower than ever. They were no longer taking enjoyment in feasting, singing or the music of the harpers. Such a pall of fear was cast over them that I was obliged to swallow my pride and send another messenger to Cuchulainn. This time I chose to send Mac Roth.

I improved my terms. On my instructions Mac Roth offered Cuchulainn the highborn women from among our captives, and all the dry cattle. He also offered him the slave women and the milk cattle. But Cuchulainn refused it all.

Then Mac Roth said to him:

'Is there any proposal that *would* be acceptable to you?'

'There is,' Cuchulainn answered, 'but you will have to find it out.'

He began putting on his tunic.

'If there is anyone in the camp who knows my terms,' he said, 'then I will abide by them. If not, don't bother to send any more messengers to me.'

As he strode off he called over his shoulder:

'Tell Medbh if she sends anyone else to me with any more of her terms I'll kill him!'

When I heard all this, I went straight to Fergus.

'I know what the terms are,' he said, 'but I can't see that they are of any advantage to you.'

'Let me be the judge of that,' I said, 'tell me what they are.'

'Cuchulainn's terms,' said Fergus, 'are that a single champion from among your army should go out to fight with him every day. And that during the time of combat your army may move forward, but on the death of each warrior the army must halt and make camp again until the next day.'

'This is a bad proposal!' moaned Ailill.

'On the contrary,' I replied, 'the proposal is good. For it is better to lose a warrior a day than a hundred each night.'

As soon as I had spoken Ailill said:

'Who will go and tell Cuchulainn we accept the terms?'

'Who else, but Fergus.' I said acidly.

VI

AFTER THIS agreement, instead of his sneaking, nightly skirmishes against our armies, Cuchulainn began to prove himself a more worthy opponent. But it was difficult persuading warriors to go and meet him. I was obliged to use all my wiles. I played on the vanity of some, I offered land and riches and the hand of my daughter Findabhar to others. In this way, day by day, I held off the heavy slaughter that had plagued my armies.

During this time I took out a third of my troops and went north to secure the Don. We captured him quite easily, but it was no easy thing to bring him back. All the way the huge animal kept bucking, careering and fighting. Nevertheless we managed it.

Cuchulainn was extremely angry when he heard about it. I think he considered it the greatest insult of the entire war. It was shortly after that he broke the pact and killed Ferbaeth treacherously with a holly spear the night before their combat.

After that we broke the pact, too. We began sending out warriors each night to try and kill him, but he slew them all.

Because of this I had to taunt the next warrior, Loch into going. Loch was one of our most skilled fighters. He met Cuchulainn at the next ford and came very close to defeating him, but Fergus – that snake in our ranks, sent one of the Ulster warriors, Bricriu the Poison-tongued, to jeer at him until his wrath was raised again. Even so, Cuchulainn was unable to kill Loch until he resorted to his most deadly weapon, his barbed spear, the *gae bolga.*

After that it was almost impossible to find any man who would go against him. We tried to call a truce but Cuchulainn still insisted on single combat. Then six princes, sons of the same king, offered to go together against him. But even the six were unable to withstand him and he killed them all.

Eventually, I was driven to ask Cuchulainn for another meeting. My plan was treacherous, but the man was beginning to seem inhuman and I had to preserve my troops. We met on a hill in Cronech. Cuhulainn was to come unarmed and I was to have only my troop of women with me. But Cuchulainn brought his sword and I had fourteen warriors waiting with their javelins. Even so, before my eyes, the boy Hound of Ulster killed every one.

Swallowing my pride, I tried everything after that. I offered him my daughter Findabhar, I even tried to persuade Fergus to fight against him – but all to no avail. Then I sent a whole tribe – the Clan Calatin against him. There were twenty-nine of them. This time they almost had his life in their hands, but the Ulster warriors were beginning to rise from their pangs and a stray Ulsterman came to Cuchulainn's aid. Between the two of them they slew the whole Calatin clan.

The first powerful warrior to come out of his pangs at that time was Cethern, a rash and bloodthirsty man. He came upon us alone, and rushed among our troops dealing deathblows from his chariot to left and right. I took him on myself, fierce giant that he was. I think he was surprised to see me wielding my stinging lance and raising my iron-bladed sword above him, for mine was the first great wound he suffered.

Then, while the Ulster warriors were still rising from their beds and mustering for war, trouble broke out in our army when some of the kings found out they had each been offered Findabhar for wife. It was unfortunate that they discovered this just before we joined battle, for this had been an effective strategy and had done much to secure their loyalty. Now the infighting I had managed for so long to prevent broke out and some five hundred of our men killed each other in a fit of jealous feuding. Afterwards poor Findabhar was heartbroken. I thought then, as I had thought so often before, that though she had inherited my beauty, the poor girl sorely lacked her mother's mettle.

When at last we joined battle with the army of Ulster, I knew the omens were against us. Nevertheless I led three successful raids against the Ulster army and thought our sides were well matched until Cuchulainn rose from his sickbed and joined the fray. Nevertheless, we fought on bravely, but the greatest blow to us was when Fergus and the troop of Ulster Exiles turned as one and ran from Cuchulainn. This marked the final turning of our fortune, and I found out later it had been secretly arranged between them.

In the end we had to admit defeat, but even so we had the bull and most of our spoils so there was little shame in it.

It was when we were marching back that my gush of blood came on me – my woman's fertility, and with it a great desire to make water. I am famed for this moment, for that is when Cuchulainn came up behind me and, as he claims, kept his hand from striking me. It was said afterwards that I made three great channels in the earth from my outpouring. If such a thing were true, it would make me a river-yielding goddess, indeed!

The bulls themselves, the quarrelsome powers behind this war, however, did not fare so well. They met together on the Plain at Tarbga and fought a dreadful battle to the death. The Don destroyed the White-horned and spread its body parts all over the land, but afterwards his massive bull's heart broke within him.

Once I was back in Cruachan, I tried to accept our defeat with equanimity. After all I was not completely disgraced. We had taken the bull, and we had also plundered the land, harassed its people, and brought back a ton of booty – captives, troops of horses, and countless herds of sheep and cattle.

....

IT GAVE me some pride to learn that over the next few years our so-called Great Cattle Raid began to rankle in the mind of Conchobor – that treacherous king of Ulster. It rankled enough, I learned, to keep him awake at night and make him plot revenge against us. As soon as I heard this I, too, began making plans. I knew there was really only one thing that I needed to do and that was to kill Cuchulainn. But this time, where strategy had failed before, I planned to employ magic.

I decided to use the three daughters of Calatin. They were the only children that remained of that great tribe – the twenty-nine men who were killed by Cuchulainn in one day. The daughters were misshapen, born in the shadow of their father's and brothers' deaths, and trained from birth to revenge them. So it is not true, as some say of me, that I maimed them. Certainly I encouraged them in the black arts, but their feet were already on that path.

When the time came, and with the help of the three sisters, it was an easy thing to send delusions on Cuchulainn. He was losing his strength then and his *geisa* were already breaking when we joined in battle. His death, I would say, was due more to the power of the

Morrigan than my need for vengeance. And perhaps I was just a pawn – the rock on which he finally was broken. Yet it seems fitting to me that he was defeated by a High Queen and her women.

After he died the whole of Ulster grieved him and, in my own way, too, I think I mourned his passing. For the man himself had once called me 'high and splendid Medbh'. Which is, after all, a worthy tribute from the Champion of Erin.

ARIANRHOD

Behold a bard who has not chanted yet.
But he will sing soon
And by the end of his song
He will know the starry wisdom.

THE WAVES are quiet today. Slight, light ripples like overlapping scales of an endless iridescent fish. Yes, the sea is playful today, busily fish-washing my little island. But yesterday it reared like a lion, leaping up onto the rocks then slithering down, an endless sugary glaze.

Ah the sea is sweet! I like its sweetness, and I like the wildness of the water. At night I stand barefoot on the rocks, my starry crown like a silver wheel about my head, the wind fingering my moon-white robe. By day, the sea is like a tumbled cloak of blue-black sammet, spreading from my shoulders to the ends of the world.

My castle, *Caer Sidi,* stands in the middle of my island, ringed by rocks. Rising between its turrets is a shining tower of glass. As the seasons pass they play my tower like a flute. The sun strikes bright-toned crystals from it, the wind lips and shrills its sullen tune, the rain weeps against it then veils it from human sight. And all the while the tower turns. Imperceptibly. Like the year.

And I turn too, within my tower. In spring I am virgin – 'a chaste white-armed maiden,' luring and alluring, desiring and desired. Mermen come in the licking of the waves and give me water-children. In the hot heart of the year I yield my bounty – child or fruit, corn or wreaths of flowers. Then, when the earth's delights lie hidden in the grave of the year, I set the tests and store my wisdom. Turn and turn again. The endless round – the radiant, ravishing, rough and richness of the land!

Come the sweet spring I rise again as maid.

I am known as one of the most beautiful women of the land. This is my story.

It was on a fish-wash day like today that he first came – Gwydion my magic brother. He came spinning towards me, oars like elongated arms whirling his boat across my rippling, blue-robed waves. Soon, I knew, he would hold me in his arms.

But it was not just me he came to visit. It was my turning chair, my magic bower at the heart of my castle, the poet's secret seat of fire.

He came into shore and tied the boat. Then he began climbing the steep pathway to my caer. How long since I last saw him? Three years or more. Yet it seemed as if an age had passed, a slip of time between the worlds. His eyes were different, his pupils blue-black spirals. I could see new magic in them – furtive, feral. He held me close against his breast. Sun and moon were we together. Moon and sun.

I drew apart from him and looked again into his eyes. I thought I caught in them the flick-switch of a tail, a fleshy snout, scent-flared.

'I have passed the tests,' was all he said.

But later, as we dined, he told me how he and our brother Gilvaethwy had been turned into wild creatures. It was Math's doing – Math our uncle, the Arch Mage, ruler of Gwynedd. As he spoke, Gwydion was reaching back into shadowed memory, his eyes darkening.

'After Math first struck us with his wand,' he said, 'we were stag and deer together.'

As he told the tale I saw them, my two brothers, treading the woods with long and elegant limbs, quivering at human noise. Gwydion was the stag, his antlers pricked out like rays of sun, crowned as Cernunnos, the horned god. I saw him weaving between thin-stemmed trees, planting false prints, vanishing in the shake of a bush, then doubling back. I could see the furtive cunning in his face. Quick-witted Gwydion he'd become. The wily bard.

'After a year,' he said, 'we returned to Math's court, Gilvaethwy and myself, with a fawn behind us. And, for a brief moment, Math turned us back to men.'

His eyes were different now. I could see a sudden softness in them.

'When Math struck us with his wand a second time,' he said, 'we became sow and boar together.'

As he told me the second story, I imagined my brothers transformed again. But now Gilvaethwy was the fierce, snout-bristled boar, and Gwydion the smooth-skinned sow. Gwydion was the fecund one, the many-breasted nourisher. Also the creature of the threshold, guardian of the gateway to the Underworld. I saw him close-snuffling the earth, seeking out the sacred mysteries, entering the goddess' womb of hidden wisdom.

Gwydion sighed as if with deep longing. He said:

'When a year had passed, we returned to Math with a piglet behind us. Then he touched us with his wand and turned us back to men.'

Wild and wary his eyes were now, and filled with cunning.

'When Math struck us a third time, we became wolf and bitch.'

Again I saw the two of them, Gwydion the he-wolf with Gilvaethwy his bitch. Two pairs of eyes, hard-rimmed, white-speckled, two sleek heads tilted in the white wheel of the moon. I heard their fearful, Otherworldly howls. How far had they travelled, I wondered, four-footing the slender ridge, the dappled edge between the realms? Far into dreams and shadows, weaving between the dark of death, and life's awaking.

Gwydion's voice brought me back from my reverie.

'When the year was up,' he said, 'we returned to Math's court with a cub behind us. Then Math turned us back to men, and our three offspring became young boys. Our tests were finished. He sent us to wash and dress ourselves and then he invited us to join his council.'

I looked at my brother.

'When did all this happen?' I asked.

'After the ravishing of the virgin.'

There was silence between us. The ravishing was a hard thing to understand. A young virgin, Goewin, had been Math's footholder, as was the custom. But Gilvaethwy, seeing her every day sitting patiently with Math's feet in her lap, began to burn with longing for her. Seeing this, Gwydion had hatched a plot to start a war. When Math rode out to battle, Gwydion stole back to court with his brother and held off the waiting women while Gilvaethwy raped her. Their three years of living as animals was meant to be their punishment. Clearly Gwydion did not see it like that.

As if he could read my thoughts, Gwydion said:

'Goewin is now Math's wife.' He looked hard into my eyes as if pleading with me to understand. 'It was time for the Virgin to become the Mother.'

I said nothing, but my hand shook as I poured wine into his bronze goblet.

'Our transformations were our shamanic testing,' said Gwydion, raising it to his lips. 'And now you know why I have come.'

He put down his goblet. Again there was silence between us. At last I said softly:

'Math must need a new footholder.'

Gwydion smiled.

II

NEXT DAY I travelled with Gwydion to the court of Math the Arch Mage, our uncle – he who could hear the words and whispers of his people carried to him on the wind.

I was officially appointed as Math's virgin footholder. The *geis* upon him was such that except when he rode his horse to war, he could not live without me. Thus his feet were always in my lap. And my lap was the seat of his power. My white arm held his sleeping head at night. My dark hair with the auburn embers glowing in it, my maiden energy, lent his hoary wisdom the strength of youth. When the time came for him to test my virgin power, I bowed to his request. I yielded to the ritual. Dressed in my finest gown of midnight blue with a covering robe of virgin white, I processed along the length of the Great Hall. I met Math face to face. I waited as he laid his staff on the ground. Then, in full view of the court, I stepped over it.

I do not know if the child came from Gwydion or from the potent staff of Math. Sacred children have magical and uncertain parentage. But when I stepped over Math's wand, first I birthed the mer-child, Dylan, son of the wave, who afterwards wriggled free at his naming in the water. Then, as I ran back down the hall, something else fell from me, a tiny scrap of life that needed all of Gwydion's arts to raise into being.

While the scrap of child lay hidden in the dreaming wisdom of Gwydion's oak chest, I went back to my tower. Some say I fled in shame. It is not so. Certainly the Goddess knows humiliation. Certainly there came a time when she was used as child-bearer, a time when she was parted from the sacred son. And I, too, was deliberately disgraced and parted from my son. I suffered pain, humiliation and a four-years' penance before I saw him again. Such was Rhiannon's fate. And such was my fate, too.

But although denied care of him, I knew I could still use my power of initiation on my child.

III

AFTER I returned to Caer Sidi, I guarded the secret flames of my poet's bower and saw the seasons round. Three times my tower made its annual turning. And then it was the fourth turn - and the season of the crone....

During the four years my son was under Gwydion's care, he was wet-nursed and then fostered at Math's court. He grew fast as such magic children do, and soon seemed twice his age. Then one sharp-sunned morning just before the dark season took hold, a boat came in view again, my blue-eyed brother and the boy within it.

'May the gods prosper you!' Gwydion called as they ascended the path.

'Who is the boy that follows you?' I asked.

'A son of yours,' he replied.

'Why have you humiliated me?' I said in answer. 'Why have I been kept in disgrace for so long?'

'Your disgrace is a small thing,' replied my brother, 'if it's caused only by my rearing so fine a boy as this.'

I looked at the boy. I saw at once the essence of him, and his destiny.

'What is the boy's name?' I asked.

'He does not yet have one,' answered Gwydion.

A look passed between us.

'Then this is his fate – that he shall have no name until I give him one!'

Gwydion saw the dark power rising in me.

'If you are angry because you are no longer virgin,' he said, 'remember this. Whatever you do, the boy *will* receive a name!'

Then he took the boy and left my castle.

IV

I HAVE never understood why men fear the dark face of the goddess. For it is the time of sleep and closing, the time of contemplation, of searching for the unseen treasures, the time of dream and making when all things seem possible. Out of it comes her deep, reviving wisdom, and her challenging. Perhaps this is what men fear – and yet it is her challenging that empowers them.

There were three challenges I had to put upon my son. Three tests. And whether Gwydion realized it or not, he played into my hands.

Next morning when I rose, my servants came to tell me that two shoemakers had arrived by boat – a man and his young apprentice. They told me their shoes were of a rare quality, made of beautiful Cordovan leather rubbed with gold. So I sent a servant down with the measurement of my feet.

When he brought the shoes back they were exquisite. I tried them on but found they were slack at the heel. So I sent them back and asked for another pair to be made. But this time, when they were brought up to me, I found they were too tight. My servant went down to the harbour and told the shoemaker that he had blundered again.

'Then let her come down herself that I may see her feet,' was the shoemaker's reply.

As I approached the harbour I saw a man cutting out the shoes and, beside him, a boy apprentice sitting in the boat, stitching them.

'I am surprised you were unable to make my shoes the right size,' I said.

'Lady,' replied the man, 'Now that you have come yourself, they will be perfect.'

He took my arm and steadied me as I climbed into the boat. When I was seated, he lifted the heel of my foot and set his measuring rod against it. While he was doing this I looked at the boy. He had stopped stitching and had taken up his little sling. A wren had just alighted on the side of the boat. The boy took aim and hit it neatly in the leg.

'Well-aimed, Fair One of the sure hand!' I exclaimed.

As soon as I had spoken, the illusion fell from the man and the boy. The blue eyes of my brother met me, his face changed shape, as did that of the boy. I saw that they were Gwydion and my son.

'Ha!' Gwydion cried triumphantly. 'Now you have given him a name, one that will do well enough! Lleu Llaw Gyffes he shall be called from now on, Lleu of the Skilful Hand!'

Gwydion thought I was angry as I turned my face into the spray. But ah, the child was so young! By shooting the wren the boy had unknowingly revealed his destiny and I, his mother, named him for it. I knew what the boy could not have known – that the wren was once named the king of birds, having outwitted the eagle. And, because of that, each winter solstice the wren undergoes a ritual sacrifice.

I turned on Gwydion and cried accusingly:

'What makes you think you will serve your cause better by hurting me!'

Gwydion looked at me in exasperation.

'I haven't begun to hurt you yet!' he spat out in reply.

Mistrust and tension were mounting between us. I was angry because I was fearful for the boy. The calling of the sacred king is high. It is a bitter destiny. Such a destiny was to fall upon my son.

I climbed ashore and faced Gwydion and Lleu as they sat watching me from the boat. I raised my voice. My robes were billowing about me.

'Then this is the second fate concerning the boy,' I cried. 'I swear that he shall never take up arms until I arm him!'

A shiver ran through me as I spoke, for I knew how the boy would be killed.

'And I shall never do that!' I said.

But even as I said them, my last words were taken by the wind and whirled into blackness.

V

IT WAS a few years later that the two poets came to my island. I welcomed them, for it was good to hear new tales. In celebration, a special feast was prepared that night and there was great excitement within the castle at their coming. As we sat at meat, the younger bard came forward and offered to tell us news from the shore and the latest tales of the land. Then he sat on a low stool and tilted his harp until it was lying against his shoulder. His tales were witty enough and he plucked at his harp quite prettily. Besides that, his good looks were a delight to the women. After he had entertained us, there was a short lull and then the older bard took over. I had been conversing with him most of the evening, and there was something about his eyes that held me, something about the mellow tone of his voice that stirred my memories. When he took hold of the harp, a hush fell on the company. Even before he set his fingers to the strings, it was evident he was master of his craft. As he played, the dropped notes fell into the hall like water dripping in a pool, the music fanning out, catching us in its spell. Had he put a glamour on us, I wondered? For now the sounds were bright as flames, licking about our walls, their long tongues pulling us into the past as the bard sang of old battles, high deeds, the glory of the hero. While he sang, a rapt look came on the young bard's face, a fevered longing. I wondered then if he had chosen the right profession.

We caroused long into the evening until, finally, the fire was covered and we left the hall for the night. I went up to my chamber and for a long time I lay on my couch unable to summon sleep. The old tales had hold of my mind, my blood was fired with the deeds of the heroes, their high daring, the battle cries, the deaths, the cost, the glory of it all. At last, to rid myself of the fever, I got up and climbed the stairway to my tower. It was cool and clear as I looked out. Pricking through the silk blackness were piercings of bright light. I looked up and saw the Corona Borealis – my own crown, throbbing with power. I looked down and far below I saw the starlight fall like ragged cloud upon the water. I turned within my tower and, as I turned, I caught a sudden flick of movement – a long sleeve, wind-flapping like a wave. I stared and then I saw it again. At the same time I saw a line of liquid silver running down a rod and, beside it, a head thrown back. I knew the rod. It was a mage's wand. I watched it for a while and tried to understand its movements. Then I went back to my bed and lay there, in a state of agitation, until dawn.

I rose at first light and looked out again. And now I saw the effect of the conjured magic. A fleet of ships was spread out around my island. There was blaring of trumpets and the bustle of preparation as if for attack.

I ran barefoot to the bards' chamber and knocked on the door.

'Open up,' I cried. 'Please help me!'

The young bard opened the door. I rushed in and thought I caught a look of cunning on the older poet's face.

'This is not a safe place!' I cried.

The old bard stirred on his couch:

'What is it?' he asked. 'I can hear sounds of trumpets and commotion.'

'We are under attack,' I said, 'A fleet has surrounded us!'

The two men stared at me.

'The sea is so thick with them we can barely see the colour of the waves!' I cried. 'And they are moving fast towards us. What shall we do?'

'Lady,' said the elder bard, throwing on his tunic. 'There is nothing we can do but close up the fort and defend it as best we can.'

'I have arms,' I said.

'Then go and fetch them,' he commanded. 'and bring some for the lad.'

I hurried off and came back with my maid. We were carrying two sets of arms between us.

'Lady,' said the bard, 'while I arm myself, would you arm the lad, for he has less experience of battle.'

I looked at the youth and saw the same light in his eyes, the same glow as when he had heard the tales. I began to arm him.

When I had finished, a voice spoke behind me.

'Have you finished?'

'Yes,' I replied.

'Then,' said the voice again, 'we can disarm ourselves.'

'But the fleet ... ' I began, then broke off.

'Lady, there is no fleet outside!'

The voice was familiar now. I turned, and there before me was my brother Gwydion, a look of triumph on his face. Beside him stood Lleu, my son, garbed in armour, and almost trembling with joy.

'And now,' laughed Gwydion, 'the boy has his arms!'

Fear rose in me and, with it, anger:

'By all the gods, you are an evil man,' I cried. 'Any boy could have lost his life against the fleet you conjured today!'

It was a moment's weakness – the cry of a mother wanting to keep her son from war. But deep within me I knew he had earned his arms, for I had seen his courage. I also knew that from this day onwards Lleu would carry a spear. And, though the spear would be his chiefest glory, it would also be the death of him. I knew all this and feared for him in my heart.

Now my son had passed two tests and there was one remaining. As Gwydion and Lleu were winding their way down towards my harbour, I lifted my arms. I was standing barefoot on a dark mass of rock. Like Gwydion with his wand, I raised my arms and spoke these words across the ocean:

'This is the third destiny concerning my son!' I cried. 'He shall never marry a mortal woman! He shall never wed a woman of the race of men!'

I saw them turn, stark-faced. They could see my tunic with its long sleeves flapping like birds' wings, my white robe lifting behind me like a bridal train. They might even have glimpsed the wheel of silver circling my brow. But Gwydion was shaking his fist at the rocks and water, spitting out words for the wind to wrap and carry to my ears:

'You always were an evil woman!' he shouted, 'And no one in their right mind should serve you!' He jerked the tethering of the little boat. Then he turned and raised his wand:

'Lleu *will* have a wife,' he shouted, 'whatever you swear upon him!'

In spite of his anger, I smiled as I made my way back into my castle. Already I knew that Gwydion would outwit me. I knew that, with the aid of Math, he would create a wife for Lleu. I also knew that, though she would cause him pain, she would still be the right wife, the only wife that Lleu could possibly have. For, being the sacred king, no mortal woman could be his consort. He would have to wed the land itself.

That night I dreamed. And in my dream I picked a spray of meadowsweet, I ran my hand across the broad bole of an oak, I walked amongst the waving hues of broom. I looked up and saw two nippled hills against the sky, a deep ravine between two fallen boughs and, in the woods, a tangle of white-flecked ivy like unruly strands of hair.

And then, far off, I heard a twittering laugh.

CERIDWEN

MOUNTAIN MOTHER am I, Cauldron Keeper, Great Goddess of the Lake.

My home is in Lake Tegid where my house rests on the heart of the waters. In its deepest chamber lies the cauldron, chief and richest treasure of the whole land. Its mouth is large enough to swallow up a man, its belly big enough to hide him. White pearls dance upon its rim like shining teeth.

Mother am I and Wise One. And my wisdom is this: that dark and light are equal, the dark being but a cloak that hides the light. And my knowledge is this: that the power of night is found in birthing day, and the power of winter in begetting spring, and the power of death in bringing forth new life.

And now let me tell my story.

When I first lived in Lake Tegid, I was married to Tegid Voel – Tegid the Bald, by whom I had two children. The first child that I bore was of the night. His eyes were two dark shadows when he left my womb. I called him Morfra, meaning Black Crow, but afterwards I made his name Avagddu, 'Utter Darkness'. The child was black as cavebound darkness. But I nursed him, fearsome and misshapen as he was, and kept my counsel.

The next child tumbled from my womb with golden hair and eyes like dewdrops. This child was of the light and pulled the honeyed sun behind her, so I called her Creirwy, meaning Dear One.

Day and Night, my children, Dark and Light – the foundation of my wisdom.

When they were nearly grown, I visited my cauldron where it waited for me, vast and empty.

First I called the element of air, the power of knowledge, and I heard a rushing wind pass through the chamber.

Then I called the element of water, unseen wisdom, and I heard it flow into the chamber.

Then I called up fiery inspiration, and it flamed into the room and lit my candles.

Then I left the house and went into a field where I gathered nuts and berries, herbs and grasses, also creeping creatures from the earth – as the magic books instructed me.

The Books of Wisdom that I have are the Books of the Fferyllt. These were the Druids of an ancient Place of Learning in the mountains of Eryri. After their school was gone their Books of Magic found their way to me, the Old One, Woman of the Mountains. They have served me well. I know their *ogham* symbols and their incantations. Yet the greatest spell awaited my attention. By it I could summon up the sacred seed of wisdom, the elusive *awen*. This was now my task.

The preparations of the brew I followed to the letter, gathering potent herbs and grasses under their favoured quarters of the moon. Then I took the bones of birds and creatures of the night and beat them to a pulp and mixed it with the crush of herbs – a sweet aroma with an under-smell of rankness. Black water from the well, red water from the spring, green water from the river made the matrix for the brew. And, as a sign of Creirwy, I added a feather of the Golden Eagle, and a Crow's wing for Avagddu, such things being symbols of the Wisdom.

All the while I had the great pot stirred, to keep the liquid moving freely. For this task I had the blind man Morda stir the precious potion both by day and night. And when he took his ease, the boy who led him, Gwion Bach, took up the ladle.

A slip of a lad was little Gwion, with a shrewd look to him. A sly one, I thought, but yet there was a mystery about him.

At Lammas we began the brewing. Corn was being scythed and sheaves were rolled and stacked together. Husks were lying on the lake. It was the Season of the Mother.

Then came the festival of Samhain. After the gate was opened and the spirits of the dead had entered, came the time of death, the withering. But even in the hardening ice, I went about by night to do my secret gathering, as the Book instructed. It was the Season of the Crone.

Imbolc, the early springtime, cracked the ice and brought the damp-skinned lambs protesting from their mothers' wombs – and all the while the ladle pounded round the dwindling potion.

Beltaine brought the carefree Maiden to the time of mating. Branches were licked with tongues of leaves and splashed with blossom.

As Lammas-time drew near again, I waited. Knowing the brew was almost done, a heartbeat from the birthing, a hair's breath from the raising of the *awen*.

Whatever men say of me in later years, this secret magic wrought by me in my wisdom, was never just a foil for my Crow-black son to give him special Knowing.

Then it was Harvest time again. A year had passed. Little Gwion of the shrewd eye stirred the pot. And one day, only, waited.

But while my back was turned the black-mouthed cauldron spat the essence of the brew a day too early. The three drops leaped up into the air and landed on the young boy's thumb. I felt their force, their burning touch – what the boy's quick tongue had tasted in an instant. Now the virtue of the brew was gone.

> The first drop was the drop of Knowledge,
> The second was the drop of Wisdom
> And the third the drop of Inspiration.

Then with a great cry the Cauldron cracked in two, the echo of it ran all round the crags and valleys. But the remaining potion flowed into the neighbouring land where the horses of King Gwythno drank of it and perished.

After that, they say, I took the form of hag and armed myself with vengeful anger, I called the old man, Morda, to account and hit him so his useless eye fell from its socket, then I started out in murderous pursuit of Gwion who had stolen my son's potion.

That is not how it was.

Yet it is true that I became the Crone, the Wise One, the Initiator. And so in Crone form I pursued the fleeing Gwion down the valley.

First I pushed him to embrace the earth – a swift four-legged creature running for his life, so that he shape-changed to a hare and took on paws and fur, a soft snout, silken ears and thread-thin whiskers. Soon he heard me snapping at his heels, as I became a black-hued greyhound.

Then I chased him to a stream where, jumping in, he lost his fur and, covered now with scales, embraced the current, tumbling in its force. But soon enough he saw my otter-shadow plunging after him.

Then I chased him up into the air – he broke the water's surface, flexed his fins and stretched them into wings. Up he soared and flew across the land in feathered freedom. Then I became a hawk, and harried him through air to touch the sun's fire-ripened grain – the fruit of Lammas harvest. Down he fell, wind-carried as a tiny seed of wheat, and still I followed him, marked where he landed, then became a hen, black-plumaged with a crest of red. I dipped my beak upon the ground and swallowed him.

But the seed fell in my womb and I was Mother now a third time.

When he was born, the third eye on his brow was full and shining.

They said I planned to kill him. The truth is it was hard not to keep him. But the gods decreed, and so I put the chosen one, the bright one with the seed of knowing in him, in a leather bag of crane-skin and I sent him rocking out to sea inside a coracle.

With that my task was ended.

But the three drops of his second birth had laid on him the *awen*. And so he became like the Salmon of Knowledge, and swam into a net. That was how the young prince Elphin, son of Gwyddno, caught him.

Thus did the great Bard Taliesin have his magical rebirthing.

That is the extent of my tale. As for Taliesin, you must read of his deeds and hear his prophecies yourself.

Now that I am old, I no longer live in the lake, but in the mountains of Eryri, and the dragons of Beli pull my chariot.

BRIGHID THE CRONE

Early on Bride's morn
Shall the serpent come from the hole.
I will not harm the serpent,
Nor will the serpent harm me.

I AM Maiden, Mother and also Wise Woman. As Wise Woman I went into the darkness and now I wait there in my Crone-form. And while I wait my name is sung throughout the ages. And my flame is kept alive by nineteen maidens tending my ashless fire.

For I am the ancient goddess who waits in the darkness, the goddess who never dies. And in my two hands I hold the snakes of wisdom, curling about my fingers, their tight tongues flickering - symbols of new life, waiting to resurrect.

The gift of poetry is mine, and inspiration. Also the secrets of the seer. Power of prophecy I have, and foreknowledge. Curling my palm and looking through its 'pipe' I see the things that are to come.

For I was the lawgiver, and will be again.

I was the enabler of women and will be again.

I was the originator of the whistle in the night for the protection of women.

I was the midwife of the child of light and will be again.

I was the peacemaker between men and women and will be again.

I was the bridge between faiths and will be again.

For through my 'pipe' I see the King of Life who teaches wisdom by the well.

I was born at sunrise when my mother put her foot over the threshold.

I was born neither outdoors nor in, neither in the daytime nor at night.

I stand at the point between the worlds.

And I am no sweet-milk goddess, for I wield the powers of fire and water, and raise my flaming torch against the cave of night.

But soon I shall rise from the realms of darkness, like the serpent from its hole. Then I shall wake the spring, and bless the harvest, and become the Corn Queen. And again I shall close the circle and become the Crone.

But then I shall become the maid again and bring the blessings of my wells and waters, my milk and my dew. And I shall save the Mabon, the sacred son. I shall save him by my fire, and by the ring of flames that burns above my head. The ring of flames that dances with the seasons.

For I am Brighid, born at the rising of the sun. I am Brighid who was bathed in milk. My breath revives the dead, oil is poured upon me, a fiery pillar rises above my head – the fire of the goddess Brighid that flares up to the heavens and can never be put out.

Notes on Stories

The Sources of the Myths

THE EARLIEST recorded source of the Irish myths is the *Book of the Dun Cow* dated 1106 which includes the famous *Tain Bo Cuailnge* or 'Cattle Raid of Cooley' telling the exploits of Cuchulainn and known as the Ulster Cycle. Other manuscripts include 'The Yellow Book of Lecan' and 'The Book of Leinster', both 14th century. Contained in these are the *Leabhar Gabhala*, or Book of Invasions, the *Dinnsenchas* or Place Name stories and the Fenian Cycle which tells of the heroic deeds of Finn and the Fianna.

The Welsh manuscripts are slightly later in date than the Irish, the main ones being the White Book of Rhydderch (c.1325) and the Red Book of Hergest (c.1400) from both of which the stories of the *Mabinogion* were compiled. The *Mabinogion* begins with four great tales or 'branches', which are considered to be the Mabinogi proper. A further seven stories were included by Lady Charlotte Guest when she translated and compiled the volume in 1849.

The Maiden Goddesses

Brighid the Maiden

BRIGHID IS the Maiden who opens the year. She is arguably the greatest and most enduring of the Celtic Goddesses (see also The Morrigan) Although considered primarily a Spring Maiden and a fertility goddess, she has also been invoked down the ages as protective Mother and powerful Seer. Because of this, she provides a blueprint for the three great archetypes. She is therefore the goddess that overarches all the other goddesses in this book. She has undergone the suffering of the Mother and has reached the wisdom of the Seer. Yet she is ever young and can be invoked as a close companion and guide on the Goddess' Journey.

Both in Celtic and mediaeval times Brighid was worshipped at the Festival of Imbolc on February 1st. This festival was marked by young girls dressed in white who processed with Brighid's image in the form of a corn doll. Imbolc is observed today by lighting candles to bring in Candlemas, the Celtic New Year, and making corn cakes, corn dolls and plaited crosses in Brighid's honour.

The verse quoted is a traditional New Year invocation, now turned into a carol. The invocation comes from two traditional poems, 'Praises of Brigit' and 'Blessing of Brigit' found in *Carmina Gadelica*.

BLODEUWEDD

THE STORY of Blodeuwedd appears in *Math, Son of Mathonwy*, which is the Fourth Branch of the *Mabinogion*.

Blodeuwedd represents the land and her function is to keep the cycle of the seasons turning. At the core of this myth lies the ancient ritual of the king being wedded to the land and undergoing his annual sacrifice. This is linked to the motif of the summer and winter kings fighting for the hand of the spring maiden, and typically overcoming each other in turn at the solstices. It is this theme that underlies the many Celtic and medieval tales of triangular love affairs. Thus, when she becomes the agent of Lleu's death Blodeuwedd is enabling him to fulfil his destiny. Likewise when Lleu turns her into an owl, he is helping her move to her next phase – that of Wise Woman or Crone. Seen from the impersonal perspective of nature, these apparent betrayals are cyclical truths concerning the turning of the seasons and the need for renewed fertilization.

On May 1st the Celts celebrated the coming of spring with the Festival of Beltain. This was a festival of fire and fertility and is the origin of the May Day festivities, which are still observed today.

BOANN

THE STORY of Boann is found in the 12th-century *Dinnsenchas*, or 'History of Places'.

Boann is the ancient Goddess of the River Boyne, the most magical river in Ireland. She was one of the Tuatha de Danaan, the People of the *Sidhe*. Because of her connection with the Well of Segais, she was also Patron of Poetry, Preserver of Wisdom and Guardian of the Source of Knowledge. The sacred well of Segais was surrounded by nine hazel trees that dropped their 'Hazelnuts of Inspiration' into its waters. Five salmon lived in the waters and ate the nuts. These were the famous Salmon of Wisdom. The symbolism of the well with its hazelnuts and Salmon of Wisdom was central to Celtic belief, for it represented the sacredness of poetic inspiration. Fish – of which the Salmon was considered the most ancient, were connected with ancient feminine wisdom, because they inhabited the sea, the realm of the Great Mother.

Beside the Boyne stands the impressive megalithic passage tomb of Newgrange. On the morning of the Winter Solstice on December 21st the first rays of the sun strike through an aperture above the opening and illumine a chamber deep within. This penetration of the womb of the Goddess Boann by a ray of the sun heralded new birth.

SABRINA

THE STORY of Sabrina is found in 'History of the Kings of Britain' by
Geoffrey of Monmouth.

The River Severn is Britain's longest river, rising in the Welsh
mountains at Plynlimon and running for 220 miles down to the Bristol
Channel. It is characterized by the famous 'Severn Bore' a phenomenon
caused by the tide backing up from the Bristol Channel for several miles
along the river. This gives rise to an extraordinary and impressive tidal
wave – sometimes as much as a meter high – that sweeps along the
lower reaches of the Severn and produces a sudden swell between its
narrower banks. The Bores usually occur within one to three days
following a new moon.

Estrildis and Sabrina are a mother/daughter duo. There are
strong hints of ancient matriarchal worship running throughout this
tale and Locrinus himself appears to be caught between acknowledging
the old devotion to the Goddess and subscribing to the new patriarchal
cult of the hero. Whereas Estrildis, symbolic of the old order, perishes
in the river, Sabrina takes on its nature and commands it, making it her
own. The story suggests that goddess worship may have gone
underground and continued in secret for a time before patriarchal
religion finally took over. But, at the end of the story, we are left with a
sense that Sabrina has somehow transformed her controlled and stifled
life into personal triumph. In giving her name to the river she lays claim
to one of the most important life-giving arteries of the landscape and
ensures that her memory can never die.

THE MOTHER GODDESSES

DEIRDRE

THE STORY of Deirdre is found in a 9th-century Irish text and was included as a tale in the *Tain Bo Cuailnge* – the famous 'Cattle Raid of Cooley'.

Deirdre is a powerful and well-known figure in Irish mythology. She demonstrates great strength and humanity as well as the ability to discern treachery and foresee the future. She is the dishonoured Goddess who will not bow to circumstance. She is dishonoured because she is not allowed the consort of her choice, nor is she allowed to fulfil her own destiny. Yet throughout her tale she stands up for her right to sovereignty. More than this, she challenges the code of the Irish hero when she criticizes Fergus for putting his obedience to his *geis* before his pledge to protect the Sons of Usna. Her story also reflects the theme of the summer and winter kings fighting over the goddess (see Blodeuwedd).

The dishonour suffered by Deirdre puts the fertility of the land at risk. But there is a purity about her suffering. In weeping over her dead love, she is a type of *pietà* figure, prefiguring that of the Virgin Mary weeping over her dead son. Like Isis with Osiris and Horus, she belongs to the Mother/consort, mother/son cycle which is a very powerful one. In Deirdre's case the cycle is halted because she has no offspring – at least none that figure significantly in her story. This makes her suffering even more poignant. Deirdre reminds us of our humanity and the depths to which suffering can take us. She is also a powerful image of pity. At another level she demonstrates what can happen when a woman is not allowed to choose or fulfil her own destiny. The dishonoured Goddess is an eloquent figure. In her grief and childlessness Deirdre symbolizes the barrenness of the earth, plundered by man's drive for power and control.

In another version of the story, instead of dying of grief, Deirdre is forced to remain with Conchobar for a year during which she refuses to eat or look up. Eventually she is placed in a carriage between Conchobar and another suitor, and contrives her own death by launching herself from the carriage and dashing her head against a rock.

The story of Deirdre, although poignant and well known in itself, is also important because it explains how Conchobar's betrayal of the sons of Usna causes Fergus, his finest warrior, to deflect to Medbh's army in Connacht.

BRANWEN

THE STORY of Branwen forms the second branch of the *Mabinogion*. It is also the only one of the tales that has a woman's name as its title. Even so, although it is the quiet presence of Branwen that pervades the tale, it is Bran who dominates the action. The fact that they share the same name suggests that one is the reflection of the other or, perhaps, that Branwen is giving way to her brother. For, from the beginning, there are signs that Bran has taken over Branwen's role as Goddess and has become sole Guardian of the land. Unlike the giant figure of the Dagda, who is clearly the consort of the goddess of the land (see The Morrigan), Bran, for all his benevolence, appears to be something of a usurper. Nevertheless, by making himself a bridge over the River Shannon, (he was afterwards famous for the epithet: 'The Chief shall be a bridge'), he demonstrated an understanding of the humility and service such a role requires.

For her part, Branwen seems throughout the tale to share the fate of the cauldron. She travels with it to Ireland and she dies after it is shattered. Both the loss of the cauldron and the death of Branwen signal the devastation of the land.

Efnisien is a difficult character to fathom. He stands in opposition to Bran and is appalled by Branwen's marriage to Matholwch. Because the horse is so often a symbol of the goddess (see notes to Macha and Rhiannon) it seems possible that his monstrous act against the king's horses is intended to reflect the defiling of his sister. In this retelling, for dramatic effect, Efnisien's homecoming is brought forward a few days to coincide with Branwen's deflowering.

This tale of war between Britain and Ireland bound up, as it is, with the powers of the cauldron may well have links with the ancient Arthurian tale known as *Priddeu Annwn* – The Spoils of the Underworld. This is an early poem found in the sixteenth century *Hanes Taliesin* but believed to date from the ninth century. It describes how Arthur and a shipload of companions go on a quest to seize the cauldron from a place under the sea where it is guarded by nine prophetesses. Only seven warriors return from this quest, among them Taliesin and Arthur himself. Nothing is told of the fate of the cauldron, which may have been destroyed in the raid.

The image of the cauldron pervades Celtic myth. It was a potent symbol of the feminine principle, being identified with the womb and therefore with the concept of spiritual rebirth. The magical Celtic cauldron became the basis for the Holy Grail of Arthurian legend. There are strong hints of links between the two traditions in the tale of Branwen. For example, a connection has been noted between Bran – who curiously refers to himself as 'Pierced Thighs', and Bron the Fisher King whose wounded 'thighs' (a euphemism for genitals) are the cause of the wasteland.

Bran is also known as Bendigeid Vran, or Bran the Blessed. His Singing Head provides a powerful image at the end of the story. It demonstrates the Celtic belief in the magical properties of the severed head – a mysterious and sacred object also featured in the early Grail tales.

Bran's head was taken to London and buried at the White Mount facing towards France. The White Mount is believed to be the site of the Tower of London. 'Bran' meaning raven, it is interesting to note that the Tower of London is a favourite haunt of ravens. There is also a well known saying that if the ravens leave the tower, the British monarchy will fall. In spite of this, King Arthur is said to have dug up Bran's head, preferring to be the sole protector of the land himself.

Ynis Mon is the Ancient Welsh name for Anglesea.

BRIGHID THE MOTHER

BRIGHID'S STORY concerning the Second Battle of Magh Tuireadh comes from the Irish Book of Invasions (*Leabhar Gabhala*) compiled in the 12th century.

Because of his outstanding beauty, Bres conformed to the criterion of physical perfection required for Irish kingship. This is also why he had to relinquish his position while he was disfigured by boils. The split between matriarchal and patriarchal values is strongly reflected in Brighid's story, and Bres's lack of generosity and hospitality represents the barrenness of the land caused by the new patriarchal rule.

Although this is the only Celtic story concerning Brighid, many legends and folktales gathered around her after she became a Christian saint. Because she was strongly connected with birth and regeneration it is perhaps not surprising that she was carried over into Christianity. This came about when Brighid, the Celtic deity, became confused with Brighid, the Christian Abbess. These two figures together became St Brigit, or St Bride. The Abbess presided over the monastery at Kildare (*Cille Dara* – The Cell of the Oak) which had originally been the site of a druidic grove. The many post-Celtic legends and stories feature her ancient powers of fire and water. In her guise as a Christian saint, however, Brighid was confined to her Maiden and Mother roles, being linked with the Virgin Mary.

MACHA

THE STORY of Macha is another tale found alongside that of Deirdre in the *Tain Bo Cuailnge*.

Macha is a horse goddess, the Irish counterpart of the Welsh Rhiannon and the Gaulish Epona. She also represents motherhood and the fertility of the land. Besides this she is connected to ritual games and festivals and contests of skill in arms. Her so-called 'curse' played a strong part in the later war between Ulster and Connacht, and was the reason that Cuchulainn had to fight for the most part single-handed while waiting for the Ulstermen to rise from their 'pangs' (see Medbh).

There are some three other women named Macha in Irish myth. The first is the wife of Nemedh who led the Third Invasion of Ireland. This Macha prophesies the bloody outcome of the *Tain Bo Cuailnge*. The second Macha is a warrior queen who founds Emain Macha and becomes Sovereign of Ulster. There is also a Macha who is said to be a daughter of Ernmas and sister to the Morrigan. Together with Badbh and the Morrigan she stirs up strife against the Fomorians in the Second Battle of Magh Tuireadh.

Because these other Machas have often been regarded as manifestations of the same goddess, the Macha of this tale has been seen as a dark and fearful deity – particularly because of her link with The Morrigan. But if the different Machas are taken as distinct personalities, the Macha of this tale can be seen primarily as a patron of motherhood. By causing men to experience the pain of childbirth she initiates them into the universal experience of the Mother – an amazingly enlightened act, and something no other Mother Goddess has ever done.

RHIANNON 1

THE STORY of Rhiannon is found in the first and third branches of the *Mabinogion.*

Rhiannon, like Macha, is a horse-goddess. This is made clear in the myth firstly when she appears riding her horse, secondly when the birth of her child is confused with the birth of a foal, and thirdly when she has to carry guests to the palace on her back. As her name 'High

Queen' implies, she is also connected to Sovereignty. In fact the concepts of Sovereignty and of the horse-goddess are strongly linked in Celtic belief. The annual marriage of the king with the goddess in order to fertilize the land was often ritually observed by the king mating with a mare, after which he bathed in broth made from her flesh.

Rhiannon appears when Pwyll braves the power of the Mound of Arberth, which is a gateway between worlds. She rides a white horse, symbolic of the Otherworld, and is clearly not a mortal woman. She disobeys her father's wishes and chooses her own consort but has to teach him how to outwit her father and secure her in marriage. The year's gap suggests the ritual of the goddess and the seasonal round, and the combat of the two suitors also points to this. 'Gwawl' means 'light', and Pwyll is connected with Annwn, the Underworld, having become its ruler in a previous story. It seems that Rhiannon has chosen the Dark Lord of Annwn rather than the Lord of Light. But there are complex mysteries involved here. Rhiannon's inexhaustible food bag is a type of magical cauldron. It is also a type of cornucopia – a bag of abundance associated with the horse goddess Epona. In Rhiannon's story she gives the bag to Pwyll and when Gwawl climbs inside it, he finds its powers work against him. At the same time, the image of the man in the upturned bag is suggestive of a child in the womb waiting to be born. The child that Rhiannon bears is Pryderi, whose golden hair pronounces him a child of light. Thus this story may reflect the cycle of mother/consort/child (see notes to the story of Deirdre). Like the other great women in the Mabinogion, Arianrhod and Branwen, she suffers dishonour after bearing her child but, like Branwen, is later reinstated.

The theme of the Reinstated Goddess shines through this story and offers hope. She is able to use and transform her suffering to obtain greater insight and understanding. By the end of her story, Rhiannon triumphs through endurance. She is also shamanistic, able to move between the material world and the Otherworld. She presents a less poignant figure than Deirdre, perhaps because she is aware of her magical abilities. In fact, there is something lovely and fragrant about her. As well as being associated with the mare, she is also associated with birds. The famous 'Birds of Rhiannon' are a rare but particular feature of the Otherworld.

RHIANNON 2

THIS STORY is found in the third branch of the *Mabinogion,* entitled Manawydan, Son of Llyr.

Manawydan is brother to Bran and Branwen. He is also thought to be the Welsh equivalent of the Irish sea deity, Manannan mac Lir.

Manawydan's marriage to Rhiannon is arranged by her son in order to grant his friend a kingdom. This is in line with the ancient Matriarchal custom in which the king is granted custody of the land by becoming a consort of the goddess. Manawydan is, therefore, both a new type of man who uses his wit rather than his might, and one who respects the old Matriarchal ways. Throughout the tale he both serves Rhiannon and also serves the land, bringing about its recovery at the same time as he recovers the lost goddess.

Caswallawn is the son of Beli, and cousin to Bran. When Bran marched against Erin, he left his son Caradawg in charge of his kingdom, along with six chiefs or governors. But the treacherous Caswallawn stole among them under a cloak of invisibility and killed them all. Caradawg, overcome with grief at seeing a moving sword but not being able to defend the chiefs, committed suicide, whereupon Caswallawn seized the throne

After a semi-historical opening, the tale becomes increasingly fantastical and symbolic. The emptying of the land can be seen as a symbol of the wasteland – the wasting of the earth brought about by an attempt to reap vengeance on the Goddess. When Rhiannon and her son are transported to the Otherworld, they become stuck to the fountain with golden chains and a bowl. This is a type of the Well of Wisdom, and Rhiannon can be seen as a type of Modron, or eternal mother, linked with Mabon, the son. Rhiannon's immobilisation at the Fountain of Inspiration indicates an imprisonment but at the same time a magical encounter with this supreme symbol of power and wisdom.

This is a strange and magical story, which seems to encompass bands of time and to move forward into the Christian era, and perhaps beyond. In it Rhiannon - the symbol of the Restored Goddess, triumphs yet again but this time through the help of her wise consort.

THE CRONE GODDESSES

THE MORRIGAN 1

THIS STORY comes from the Irish Book of Invasions (*Leabhar Gabhala*).

The Morrigan shows us the fearful and awesome side of the Goddess. As with Blodeuwedd, she demonstrates the impersonality of the goddess as an embodiment of natural laws, and the life/death/life principle. In her dark aspect she appears either as a crow – her emblem, or as the Cailleach, the ugly, old crone figure and harbinger of death. But the Morrigan has her fair side, which is linked to cattle and the fertility of the land. In this role she presides over the engendering of life and appears as the Goddess of Fertility and Sexuality. It is in this guise that she couples with the Dagda. During the battle (The Second Battle of Magh Tuireadh or 'Moytura') she acts in typical war goddess form, but in her later prophecies she reveals a surprisingly fair face.

Although the Morrigan is considered the darkest of the goddesses in the Celtic canon, she is closely linked with Brighid, the sun goddess. These two powerful deities – who may well be mother and daughter, together express the combined forces of darkness and light, day and night, death and life, and all the dualities contained within the figure of the one Great Goddess.

The Celts believed in a life after death and in the transmigration of souls. For them death was always dissolving into life and life into death. In this respect, their understanding of the world was cyclical and circular rather than linear, and their concept of the Goddess reflected this.

THE MORRIGAN 2

THIS TALE, known as the *Tain Bo Regamma* belongs to the Ulster Cycle and comes from the Yellow Book of Lecan. It is closely related to a similar incident in the *Tain Bo Cuailnge* and provides an interesting variant on it, particularly because it reveals her link with cattle.

In this tale the Morrigan appears both as the Cailleach, or fearful Crone, and the Crow, her totem bird. But it is in her guise of alluring fertility goddess that she appears to Cuchulainn and propositions him. Yet Cuchulainn, the hero of the new order, fails to recognize who she really is. At a basic level he treats her as a Challenger, but is unable to appreciate that she is also his protector and the agent of Sovereignty, who would offer him rule over the land. By ignoring and disrespecting her power, he fails to secure her help and, instead, limits her to her darkest role – the guardian of death.

THE MORRIGAN 3

THIS THIRD tale, 'The Destruction of Da Choca's Hostel' has many points in common with 'The Destruction of Da Derga's Hostel' and also belongs to the Ulster Cycle.

Here we see the once great and all-encompassing Sovereign Goddess of Life, Death and Fertility reduced to the role of *Bean Nighe*, the Washer at the Ford – prophetess and foreteller of death. In an echo of her former self, she is still connected to kingship but, confined to her Crone aspect, she is increasingly seen only in her darkest and most fearful form. This diminishing of her former role reflects a fear of the powers of the Goddess – a strong feature of the new Patriarchal rule.

MEDBH (MAEVE)

MEDBH'S STORY is found in the *Tain Bo Cuailnge*, 'the Cattle Raid of Cooley'. The re-telling is based on the translation by Thomas Kinsella (listed in the Bibliography), also on the translation by Winifred Faraday, and that of Joseph Dunn from the transcript of Ernst Windish – both of which can be found on the web.

Queen Medbh is a powerful, larger-than-life figure. Like Rhiannon she is accompanied by birds hovering round her shoulders, which indicates that she has Otherworldly connections. Whether or not she has divine origins, she certainly represents the role of Sovereignty, for it is her 'friendly thighs' that confer kingship on her consorts. (She is said to have brought some nine kings to this state by means of her sexual ministrations). She also exemplifies the Challenger, a role central to the Crone aspect of the Goddess.

Like the other goddesses in this section, Medbh has been much maligned and misunderstood. She has been portrayed as a cruel and vengeful woman when she is merely exercising the same battle strategy and authority as any male leader in her position. As regards the contest over the bulls, it is important to remember that Celtic women who owned property were allowed to keep hold of it after marriage. This enabled them to maintain equality with their husbands, so it is not surprising that Medbh is so concerned about the balance of property between herself and Ailill. Also, in order to preserve her sovereignty, Medbh has deliberately chosen a man who will not overshadow her in wealth and who will tolerate her sexual freedom. But, beyond the question of the bulls and her own personal power, she has right on her side because she is waging war on a tyrannical and usurping king.

A closer examination of the image of the bull, however, shows that Medbh's story can be understood on many levels. The bull has long been regarded as a symbol of masculine power and virility but, curiously, it has also been regarded as a symbol of female power. This is because its horns form the crescent shape of the new moon. It is therefore a composite symbol showing the power of woman riding the force of masculinity. The two together form a potent image of fertility. Since the bull is also connected with royalty, it is the perfect symbol for Medbh.

The story of Medbh is heartening and inspiring. She stands as the last representative of the ruling power of women, a power swiftly falling into disregard. Her triumph is that, in the face of threatened disrespect and dishonour, she proves herself the equal of Cuchulainn.

The name Medbh means 'intoxication' and the sweet, honeyed drink known as mead is named after her.

ARIANRHOD

THE STORY of Arianrhod is found in the fourth branch of the *Mabinogion*. The poem at the beginning is from 'The Hostile Confederacy', found in the *Hanes Taliesin* and attributed to Taliesin. It is translated by John Matthews.

Arianrhod's story reflects all three aspects of the Goddess: Maiden, Mother and Crone, but she has been much maligned and misunderstood in these roles.

First there is the misinterpretation of her role as virgin. The Goddess as Maiden is not a figure of sexual innocence, rather she is a woman who does not belong to a man, and is free to exercise power over her sexual choices. The term 'virgin' therefore means self-ownership rather than physical purity. Seen in this light, the virginity of the goddess, which is also self-renewing, cannot be lost. Arianrhod knows this and stands on this truth. Yet she has to bear the humiliation and punishment of patriarchal condemnation based on lack of understanding. It is this conflict over her virginity, together with the struggles she experiences with her brother Gwydion, that suggests her story may chart the transition from Matriarchal to Patriarchal power.

An interesting poem cited by Caitlin Matthews in *Mabon and the Mysteries of Britain* shows that in medieval times there was a traditional variation on the tale in which it was assumed that Arianrhod held the post of Virgin Footholder for Math at least for a short period:

> 'My plaint concerning a maid is greater than
> that of Math Hen, son of Mathonwy. The
> arm of a chaste white-armed maiden was
> every night his pillow. Arianrhod white as
> snow; that man might not live without her.'
>
> Lewis Mon 1480

This traditional variation may throw some light on the abrupt way in which, according to the *Mabinogion*, Arianrhod ignominiously fails the test and never achieves the post. As it appears in the *Mabinogion*, the whole incident is tantalizingly sketchy, as if something has been left out. It is also extremely strange, especially in the light of the strong symbolism involved, and points to Arianrhod having something of a history with Math. For, although it is held by many that Gwydion is Lleu's father, the wand of Math is a very suggestive image. It has also been speculated that Arianrhod may have been confused with Goewin, which would also support the idea of her having previously held the post of Footholder.

Although there is room for much speculation here, nevertheless it is in her role as Crone that Arianrhod has been particularly maligned and misinterpreted, which is why her story is included in this section. Seen in the context of the role of the Crone, Arianrhod is not a cold-hearted goddess who curses her son, rather her curses are challenges – aspects of the Dark Goddess that are vital to the journey her son must make into sacrificial kingship. The three injunctions she lays on him have carelessly been translated as 'curses', but are defined in the original text as 'fates' or 'destinies', which allows for a very different understanding of her power.

When seen in her true light, Arianrhod emerges as an important goddess who guards the Poetic Seat of Awen and holds the key to creative inspiration. Her name means Starry Wheel and she is linked to the Northern Crown, the *Corona Borealis*. The image of the goddess with the circle of stars about her head has been bestowed on the many images of the Virgin Mary who also has such a halo and who often stands with her feet on the crescent moon. The Virgin Mary is also particularly connected with the sea and with fish. Arianrhod can therefore be seen as providing an ancient model of the Virgin Mother who births the sacrificial son – the son who is killed and hangs on a tree before being magically restored to life again.

Arianrhod is also allied to Ariadne, weaver of the cosmic web in Greek mythology. The symbols of the wheel and weaving are bound up with the idea of destiny, which is very much at the heart of this story.

CERIDWEN

THE STORY of Ceridwen comes from a 16th-century manuscript known as the *Hanes Taliesin*.

The great Celtic goddess Ceridwen has been variously called the Great Witch, the White Sow and the Dear One. She belongs to the tradition of Scottish Mountain Mothers or Cailleachs. Her two children symbolize the dual powers of darkness and light.

The cauldron is a symbol of regeneration, its brew being 'awen' or inspiration. It is also a prototype of the Holy Grail (see Branwen). Its three drops carry the same charge as the Salmon of Wisdom and, in fact, this story parallels the Irish one in which Finn mac Cumhail also mistakenly receives three drops of inspiration.

The transformations undergone by Gwion when chased by Ceridwen are of an initiatory and shamanic nature. They also reflect the four elements. The tests of the Cailleach, Witch, or Wise woman are essential to the quest for regeneration. Ceridwen's story shows us that from the dark womb of the Goddess comes the Child of Light.

Taliesin means 'Shining Child' and the child shines with Otherworldly and inspirational knowledge. When he appears to Elphin in place of the salmon catch, he symbolizes the Salmon of Wisdom itself.

BRIGHID THE CRONE

THE OPENING verse is from an ancient Gaelic hymn.

At the monastery in Kildare a fire was kept burning perpetually in Brighid's sanctuary, tended by nineteen nuns. It is thought that this ritual may be the vestige of an ancient tradition of vestal priestesses.

Bridghid's championing of women is not only spiritual but also practical. For example she is credited with the invention of the whistle, enabling women to summon help if attacked at night. She is also connected with the compilation of Irish laws known as the *Senchus Mor*, or Brehon Laws. Initially handed down orally by the druids, they were later written down and attributed to Sencha, or 'wiseman'. In many texts, however, Brighid is depicted as his mother, daughter or wife. So her connection with the laws is evident. The fact that so many of the laws concern the rights of women is testimony to her influence.

Traditional Hebridean tales also portray Brighid as midwife or foster mother to Jesus. As midwife she delivers him and places three drops of pure spring water on his brow. This possibly reflects the ancient tradition of the three drops of knowledge, wisdom and inspiration being conferred upon the Child of Light (see Ceridwen). Another tale tells how, as foster mother, Brighid wore a headdress of candles with which she distracted Herod's soldiers when they were looking for Jesus.

GLOSSARY AND GUIDE TO IRISH AND WELSH CELTIC PRONUNCIATION

As a general guide to **Welsh** pronunciation, *ll* sounds *cl* or *chl*; *dh* sounds *th*, as in 'then'; *ch* and *gh* are guttural.

In **Irish** pronunciation *b* sounds *v*; *c* sounds *g* or *k*; *ch* is gutteral, *d* sounds *dh*, as in 'then' (represented below as *dh*); *g* is a soft gutteral and sounds *gh*; *m* sounds *v*; *t* sounds *d*. *s* with either i or e before or after it, is pronounded *sh*; *th* is pronouned softly as in 'thin'; *ai* is pronounced as *a*; *ei* is pronounced as *e*.

Ailill	*Ayleel* – King of Connacht and husband of Queen Medbh
Alba	Scotland
Annwn	*Anoon* – Name of Celtic Underworld or Otherworld
Arianrhod	*Arianrod* – Gwydion' sister, mother of Lleu Llaw Gyffes
Avagddu	*Av-ugdhi* – Misshapen son of Welsh goddess, Ceridwen
Awen	Sacred Inspiration
Badbh	*Bave* – One of three war goddesses, triple-aspects of The Morrigan

Beltain	Celtic May Day Festival
Blodeuwedd	*Blod-eye-wedh* – Wife made out of flowers for Lleu
Bricriu	Called 'the Poison-tongued', Ulster hero, mischief-maker
Brighid	*Brigit* or *Breed*. Best known Irish Celtic Goddess
Brugh	*Brew* – Palace of Aengus Og beside the River Boyne. Also the site of the megalithic passage tomb of Newgrange
Buinni	Son of Fergus mac Roth
Cailcin	*Kalekin* - Tutor to Deirdre
Cantrev	A district, making up part of a Welsh province
Cathbad	*Kathvadh* – Chief Druid to King Conchobar of Ulster
Cliodna	*cleena* - one of the Three Great Waves of Erin
Conall Cearnach	A chief of the Red Branch warriors
Conchobor	*Kon-ch-ovor* – King of Ulster c. beginning Christian era
Cormac Connlonges	Exiled son of King Conchobor of Ulster
Cruachan	*Kruakan* – Royal seat of Maeve and Ailill in Connacht, also site of cave entrance to Otherworld
Crunnchu	*Kroonkee* – Husband of Macha
Cuailnge	*Cooley,* distinct in Ulster
Cuchulainn	*Ku-chull-in* – 'Hound of Culann'. Hero of Ulster cycle
Cymru	*Coomree* – Wales
Cygfa	*Keegfa* – Wife of Pryderi
Dagda	Chief god of the Tuatha de Danann

Elphin	Welsh Prince who fosters Taliesin
Emain Macha	*Evin Ma-cka* – Capital of Ulster
Englyn	Welsh verse-form
Fergus mac Roth	Great Ulster hero, defected to Connaught after Conchobor killed the Sons of Usna
Ficra	Son of King Conchobor
Fidchell	*Fi-kell* – Board game resembling chess
Finn (Fionn) mac Cumhail	*Fyun m' Cool* – Captain of the Fianna
Fomorians	Ancient giant race that once inhabited Ireland
Geis, (plural geasa)	*Gaysh, Gaysha* – Magical taboo or prohibition
Gilvaethwy	Gwydion's brother
Goewin	Math's virgin footholder
Gronwy Pebr	Gronwi Pevr. Lover of Blodeuwedd. Kills Lleu Llaw Gyffes
Gwern	Son of Branwen
Gwydion	Magician and brother of Arianrhod
Illan	Son of Fergus mac Roich
Laeg	Cuchulainn's charioteer
Levacham	*Levakam* – Druidess who raises Deirdre
Lleu Llaw Gyffes	*Chlay Chlow Geh-feth* – Magically birthed son of Arianrhod
Loegres	*Lowgres* – England
Lugh	*Loo* – Son of the Dagda, a chief of Tuatha, god of light, father of Cuchulainn
Manannan mac Lir	Tuathan sea-god
Math	King of Gwynedd, uncle of Gwydion

Matholwch	*Matholook* – High King of Erin who marries Branwen
Medbh	*Mave* – Queen of Connaught
Naisi	*Nayshee* – Husband of Deirdre
Ogham	*O'am* – Cryptic druidic language
Pryderi	Son of Pwyll
Pwyll	*Poochl* – With oo as in 'foot' – Lord of Dyfed who changed places with Arawn, Lord of Annwn
Red Branch	Ulster warrior band
Samhain	*Sowain.* Celtic Festival, now Halloween
Sidhe	*Shee* – Faerie, also burial mound or barrow
Slieve	*Sleeve* – A mountain, or mountainous district
Tain Bo Cuailnge	*Toyn Bo Cooling* – The Cattle Raid of Cooley, central epic of Ulster Cycle
Taliesin	Greatest bard of Wales
Tara	Seat of High Kings of Ireland in County Meath.
Tuatha de Danann	*Tooatha day Daanan* – Race that conquered Ireland but were overcome in turn and retreated to the faerie mounds.

SELECT BIBLIOGRAPHY

Billington, Sandra and Green, Miranda, *The Concept of the Goddess*, Routledge, 1996

Campbell, Joseph, *The Hero with a Thousand Faces,* Fontana Press, 1988

Campbell, Joseph, *The Masks of God,* Arkana, 1968

Carmichael, Alexander, *Carmina Gadelica*, Floris Books, 1992

Condren, Mary, *The Serpent and the Goddess*, Harper and Row, 1989

Cross, TP and Slover, CH, *Ancient Irish Tales*, Barnes and Noble, 1936

Eddie, S. and Hamilton, C. *Timeless Wisdom of the Celts*, Hodder and Stoughton, 1999

French, Claire. *The Celtic Goddess: Great Queen or Demon Witch?* Floris Books, 2001

Gallagher, Ann-Marie, *Way of The Goddess*, Thorsons, 2002

Gantz, Jeffrey (trans), *The Mabinogion*, Penguin, 1976

Graves, Robert, *The White Goddess*, Faber and Faber, 1948

Guest, Lady Charlotte (trans), *The Mabinogion*, Llanerch, 1990

Hamilton, Claire *Tales of the Celtic Bards*, O Books, 2003

Hyde, Douglas, *A Literary History of Ireland*, T. Fisher Unwin, 1899

Jones, Gwyn and Thomas, *The Mabinogion*, Everyman, 1949

Joyce, P.W. *Old Celtic Romances*, Longman, 1920

Jung, C.G. *Analytical Psychology, its Theory and Practice*, ARK, 1976

Jung, C.G. *Aspects of The Feminine*, ARK, 1982

Kinsella, Thomas (trans.) *The Tain*, OUP, 1969

Layton, Bentley, *The Gnostic Scriptures*, SCM Press Ltd., 1987

Markale, Jean. *Women of the Celts*, Inner Traditions International, 1986

Matthews, Caitlin and John, *The Encyclopaedia of Celtic Wisdom*, Element, 1994

Matthews, Caitlin, *Mabon and the Mysteries of Britain*, Arkana, 1987

Matthews, John, *Taliesin, Shamanism and the Bardic Mysteries in Britain and Ireland*, Aquarian Press, HarperCollins, 1991

Rolleston, T. W., *Celtic Myths and Legends*, Senate, 1994

O

is a symbol of the world,
of oneness and unity. O Books
explores the many paths of wholeness
and spiritual understanding which
different traditions have developed down
the ages. It aims to bring this knowledge
in accessible form, to a general readership,
providing practical spirituality to today's seekers.
For the full list of over 200 titles covering:

- CHILDREN'S PRAYER, NOVELTY AND GIFT BOOKS
  - CHILDREN'S CHRISTIAN AND SPIRITUALITY
    - CHRISTMAS AND EASTER
      - RELIGION/PHILOSOPHY
        - SCHOOL TITLES
      - ANGELS/CHANNELLING
      - HEALING/MEDITATION
    - SELF-HELP/RELATIONSHIPS
    - ASTROLOGY/NUMEROLOGY
      - SPIRITUAL ENQUIRY
  - CHRISTIANITY, EVANGELICAL
    AND LIBERAL/RADICAL
      - CURRENT AFFAIRS
      - HISTORY/BIOGRAPHY
  - INSPIRATIONAL/DEVOTIONAL
  - WORLD RELIGIONS/INTERFAITH
    - BIOGRAPHY AND FICTION
      - BIBLE AND REFERENCE
      - SCIENCE/PSYCHOLOGY

Please visit our website,
www.O-books.net

SOME RECENT O BOOKS

TALES OF THE CELTIC BARDS
Claire Hamilton

The ancient Bards encoded their knowledge of the natural world to animals and plants and the power to heal, order and judge into teasing riddles that were told or sung, not written down. They believed they had powers of divination, shape-changing and the ability to travel to the "other world."

In this book and accompanying CD, Claire Hamilton captures the enchanting and often strange beauty of the tales they told and the music that went with them. She recreates the experience of the Celtic listeners of long ago by framing the myth with the teller, and the teller with his or her audience who would have listened spellbound as this higher knowledge was handed down.

"An original and compelling retelling of some wonderful stories by an accomplished mistress of the bardic art. Unusual and refreshing, the book provides within its covers the variety and colour of a complete bardic festival." Professor Ronald Hutton, Professor of History, University of Bristol, UK.

1 903816 54 8
£16.99 $24.95
Hardback with CD

THE CENSORED MESSIAH
Peter Cresswell

Peter Cresswell has a revolutionary new theory about the life of Jesus and the origins of Christianity. It is a thrilling story, based on modern scholarship, of how a Jewish man tried to change the direction of the religious leadership of his people. It describes a breathtaking piece of brinkmanship carried out against the Roman occupiers of Israel, a journey into the mouth of death and beyond which appeared to succeed.

Peter Cresswell is a freelance writer with degrees from Cambridge and York Universities in Social Anthropology.

1 903816 67 X
£9.99 $14.95